PROTECTION AGAINST BOMBS AND INCENDIARIES

for Business, Industrial and Educational Institutions

By

EARL A. PIKE
Captain, USMC (Ret.)

CHARLES C THOMAS • PUBLISHER
Springfield • Illinois • U.S.A.

Published and Distributed Throughout the World by

CHARLES C THOMAS • PUBLISHER

Bannerstone House

301-327 East Lawrence Avenue, Springfield, Illinois, U.S.A.

©*1972, by* CHARLES C THOMAS • PUBLISHER

ISBN 0-398-02517-7

Library of Congress Catalog Card Number: 77-190333

Printed in the United States of America

R OO-2

PROTECTION AGAINST
BOMBS AND INCENDIARIES

This book is dedicated to my associates in bomb disposal who, as members of the military or the police, daily cope with explosive and incendiary devices. They bring skill and a large measure of courage to their profession, and, because of their commitment, America can sleep a little more serenely in a time of crisis.

PREFACE

DURING World War I and for a short time
thereafter, there was a wave of bombings across the United States,
culminating in the Wall Street bombing in 1921 that killed
thirty-one people. That reign of terror was politically inspired,
attributed primarily to anarchists and Trotskyites. Now again in
America there is a breed of militant radicals who regard bombs
and incendiaries as legitimate instruments of political action —
who seek to create a new society, somehow, by the destruction of
it — to forge a new political freedom through the tyranny of
violence. As these kooks, clowns, and crazies have turned to
explosives and incendiaries, there has been an increase in the
number and in the destructiveness of this type of violence to the
point where it now approaches the proportions of a national crisis.

Because the bomb and incendiary is a new and novel threat in
our time, there are few people concerned with security in the
industrial, business, or educational communities who have the
information and experience required to effectively protect personnel and property against this type of menace. This book does
provide the specific guidelines needed to define and implement
protective measures which can reduce vulnerability to bombs and
incendiaries. Security and police personnel at all levels, business
managers and executives, and school administrators and directors
will find it a convenient guide to action in handling the bomb
threat in all its forms and manifestations.

Earl A. Pike

CONTENTS

                                            Page

Preface .... *vii*

Chapter

    I. The Threat 3
       The Prospects for Violence 3
       Target Susceptibility 11
   II. The Technology of Explosive and Incendiary Violence 14
       Explosive Bombs 14
       Incendiary Devices 42
       Employment Techniques and Destructive Capabilities 48
  III. Protective Measures 54
       Resource Inventory 54
       Physical Layout 55
       Personnel Control 60
       Training 62
       Protective Equipment 63
       Personal Protection 65
  IV. Hazard Countermeasures 66
       Planning and Preparation 66
       Bomb Threat Communications 66
       Evacuation 69
       Search 72
    V. Educational Institutions 78
       Elementary and High Schools 79
       Colleges and Universities 81
  VI. The Hospital, A Special Case 83

    Index 85

PROTECTION AGAINST BOMBS AND INCENDIARIES

I

THE THREAT

THE explosive and incendiary violence that has thus far stormed through America has already been adequately chronicled and documented. The reports published by the FBI, the McClellan committee, the House Internal Security Subcommittee, and other investigative agencies have elaborated this crisis of violence in full historical detail. Mere repetition of the many incidents that have caused death, injury, and destruction adds nothing to the record. We do, of course, find in these past experiences valuable lessons for defining workable protective procedures and measures. But we begin with the present and the future, not the past. As a prerequisite for effective security planning, we need to know the extent of the threat we face now and in the immediate time ahead — the probability of or the prospects for violence in general terms and the degree to which we, institutionally or as individuals, are specific targets.

THE PROSPECTS FOR VIOLENCE

The threat of violence is bold, bristling, and brazen in the grandiose rhetoric of the political extremists. It glares out of their language with an intensity that is chilling and a scope that is overpowering. "We must overthrow the American government," said radical campus leader Deveraux Kennedy, "and we can begin by starting '50 Viet Nams in the United States.' "

H. Rap Brown phrased it in grim and inflammatory terms, "If Americans don't come around, we're going to burn America down." There are starkly ominous dimensions in the declaration of an anonymous bomber as reported in *Look* magazine, "We are not trying to frighten the establishment; we are trying to destroy it."

3

Again and again, the commitment to violence is affirmed in parallel with a rationalization of it. "The American empire is the cruelist monster the world has ever seen," said Richard Lettau, Professor of German Literature, University of California's San Diego campus. "We must dedicate ourselves to the destruction of this empire." How could a supposedly learned man come to such a factually distorted conclusion? It is, I suppose, the result of an intellectual myopia in which the faults of our system become the entire focus of attention while the many benefits pale into insignificance. We do have faults (and we are trying to correct them), but when they are viewed in the total perspective of what the American society is, they do not add up to the "cruelist monster the world has ever seen." In fact, the historical viewpoint reveals a number of candidates for this title, but certainly not the United States.

Some may tend to dismiss all this as bombast, as blustering but empty rhetoric. It does, in a sense, ring with the frenzied hyperbole common to comic operas and Peking radio editorials. These pronouncements do, however, convey real commitment and intention. It is quite obvious to the movers of the revolution that this country must be completely destroyed, must undergo a purge of fire before social resurrection and the creation of a new humanity are possible. They perceive American society as an institution consumed by such a deep and pervasive sickness that neither surgery nor medication can arrest the malady or effect a cure. The only treatment, the only remedy of any real therapeutic value in their diagnosis is to destroy the social body completely and begin anew.

If the radicals' intentions are apparent and ominous, so too are their capabilities, and these capabilities arise from conditions that are unique to contemporary America. Even a cursory look at the evidence clearly reveals that today in the United States there exists the right combination of conditions for wide scale and extremely destructive explosive and incendiary violence. There are people in substantial numbers ready and willing to engage in violence, there are information materials in abundance on bomb construction and use, and there are large quantities of readily available explosive and incendiary supplies in a variety of forms throughout the country.

People

According to an Associated Press release, a Harris poll reports that there are 2 million people in the United States describing themselves as revolutionaries with "a readiness to use violence" to achieve their political or social goals. This is a fantastic resource for forging massive violence in any land. It only takes a team of two bombers to blow up, to physically destroy a power plant. What then is the potential for destruction of a million such teams? It literally defies the imagination. And the implications are particularly portentious in the historical context. Two million revolutionaries is a force 100 times greater than what Lenin had at his disposal when, in 1917, he siezed complete power in Russia.

This is not to say that we have 2 million people currently involved in revolutionary schemes and violent action. Were this so, we would be in a time of deadly peril in America right now. The 2 million revolutionaries exist as a resource, but it is a resource that has not as yet been effectively exploited.

There are people, however, a substantial number of people who are trying to exploit this resource. These are the radical extremists, many of whom are already engaged in violence as a political action technique, and their efforts are fostered and directed by such organizations as the RYMI (Revolutionary Youth Movement I or Weathermen), Black Panthers, White Panthers, Students for a Democratic Society, ad infinitum. These are the groups and the people whom J. Edgar Hoover collectively characterized as a "firmly established subversive force dedicated to the complete destruction of our traditional democratic values and the principles of free government . . . a new spectre haunting the Western World." And with good reason. They have achieved conspicuous successes in fomenting revolutionary ideas and ideals in America, even in spite of, at times, apparent failure.

> I see more of a civil war than a revolutionary struggle in the United States. In a civil war I believe our propaganda will be better than the pigs', and that eventually we will sway enough workers over to our side. Militarily, urban guerrilla tactics will give us a tremendous advantage over the pigs. So the civil war will be waged pretty much in guerrilla style. The whole country will become a kind of occupied

territory, and there will be an underground and real guerrillas will walk down the streets looking just like pig businessman. They will do their shit and go home and incredible things will happen at night. There will be some armed insurrection in the cities. The Bay Area will liberate itself right off and I feel that a major part of New York will be liberated. New York is really heavy. I figure a lot of cities will be divided into liberated zones and pigs' zones. And they are not going to shell them immediately because the liberals will still be screaming. And then there will be some repression for these screaming liberals and then — boom! (Statement of an American revolutionary temporarily residing in Canada [quoted in *Scanlon Magazine*])

SDS, for instance, is now an organizational wreck — splintered, fractured, split into squabbling factions by disputes of ideology and direction. In its current structural chaos, many observers have seen a failure of the SDS effort and ideological position, and they perceive in this an augury of more tranquil times to come. Such an interpretation represents a misreading of history and an unrealistic view of the present situation.

SDS has, within the context of the historical development of the revolutionary movement, been an appalling success. It has popularized among a growing minority of our people all those notions and ideas that revolution breeds and builds on. It has made our proudest traditions and ideals a heresy in our time. It has made arrogant contempt for our institutions and open defiance of our laws marks of courage and expressions of a larger wisdom. It has made all our historical experience irrelevant and all our social, political, and ecomomic achievements inconsequential. It has made subversion patriotic and treason noble. It has made violence the legitimate instrument of dissent. This is its most tragic success, that it has bred the virus of violence upon the land.

From Watts to Attica, Houston to Detroit, most of the violence is traceable to SDS'ers, Weathermen, and other revolutionaries who really don't want amicable arbitration or peaceful settlement. Their commitment to continuing violence is complete and passionate, and they have been increasingly successful in winning others to their viewpoint.

Information

The revolution, then, has people, in number and in depth of

conviction to orchestrate a theme of violence on a grand scale. And for these people, there is no lack of information on the technology of explosive and incendiary violence. It does not, first of all, require any great expertise to make a bomb. The least practical of intellects can learn the practical rudiments quite easily, and the practical rudiments are available to him through a variety of sources.

New Left Notes, the new periodical of the SDS, has frequently printed descriptions with illustrations detailing bomb and incendiary construction and usage. Such information is also found in *Quicksilver Times,* a radical newspaper published and sold in Washington, D.C. Lyle Stuart, an exploitation publisher, recently introduced the *Anarchists Cookbook,* a practical guide for contriving blast or blazes of a size compatible with any degree of revolutionary rage. On the west coast, a man named Don E. Cisco runs a thriving business selling his *New Militant's Formulary,* a do-it-yourself manual for the saboteur or terrorist. The contents of the manual include "How to make prussic acid, one shot from a water pistol into the victim's face and he is out in three seconds and dead in thirty;" "People's grenades, simple, micky mouse grenades anyone can make for pennies, yet are lethal."

The instructional material is not all indigenous in origin. It comes from a variety of foreign sources, particularly Cuba. It is true that guerilla training is available in Cuba, but, really, it is not necessary to make the trip in order to get information. A variety of instructional pamphlets on sabotage and terrorism is published there and distributed in America. Castro quite obviously has an active interest in facilitating social disruption in the United States whatever way he can. This conclusion was confirmed recently by New York City councilman Sanford W. Garelik, who was quoted by the *Washington Daily News* as saying, "The links between recent bomb incidents and Cuba's ever-boiling pot of steam for guerilla violence can be pinpointed."

We tend to think of all this material as being underground in the sense that it is distributed through covert and clandestine channels. Nothing could be further from the truth. This literal garbage flows freely and visibly throughout our society. It travels undisturbed through the U.S. mail and is hawked openly and defiantly on the street corners of the U.S. capital. It circulates unchecked on college and even on high school campuses. It is particularly prevalent in such alternative culture groups as the cultural commenses and the drug communities.

Even were this body of practical revolutionary literature not available, a person bent on violence has ready access to all the information he needs. Such standard and authoritative demolition texts as DuPont's *Blaster's Handbook* and "Explosives in Agriculture" (Institute of Makers of Explosives) are easily obtainable. Literature prepared by explosives manufacturers on how to use their products is also a good source of information for the bomber.

Explosive and Incendiary Material

For informational guidance, then, the revolutionary need not look far, nor does he find it difficult to obtain explosive and incendiary material. It is true that new, stringent legislation both at state and federal levels is making it very difficult to procure commercial explosives through legitimate channels. But there are states where such things as bulk black and smokeless powder (all you need for a pipe bomb) are not regulated and can be bought by almost anyone. And, of course, small arms ammunition, not controlled in many states, is a ready source of explosive powder for a bomb assembly.

Even if statutory controls absolutely denying access to commercial explosives should eventually be imposed, the enterprising terrorist will still be able to obtain all the explosives he desires quite easily. There are a number of explosive compounds that can be made using ingredients commonly available in drug, hardware, and grocery stores. While there is a safety consideration involved in home manufacture of most of these compounds, the revolutionaries have well demonstrated that they will not be deterred by risks.

There is very little safety risk in the high explosive ingredient that is most commonly available and most easily processed, ammonium nitrate fertilizer. It is, first of all, an excellent high explosive. An impressive, if tragic, demonstration of the destructive capability of ammonium nitrate occurred in Texas City,

Texas, where in 1948 a shipload of it blew up and killed five hundred people and leveled the town. (Not, incidentally, the worst disaster associated with ammonium nitrate fertilizer. Over 1300 people were killed in an explosion of it in Oppau, Germany, in 1823.) Secondly, ammonium nitrate can be safety processed as a high explosive by anyone. The technique requires neither great skill nor keen talent. And ammonium nitrate fertilizer is available in quantities of thousands of tons in the farming regions of America.

One other consideration of significance is that the revolutionaries are well aware of the potential of ammonium nitrate fertilizer. They have, in fact, already used it — 1700 pounds of it set up as a truck-mounted, mobile bomb at the University of Wisconsin. The result: one person killed and 6.5 million dollars damage to university facilities. There is another result. The people in the plot proved to the revolutionary community at large that with vision, daring, and a little enterprise, anyone can strike a massive blow at the establishment.

Explosives are then readily available to the extremist, and so are incendiary materials. We need not look beyond gasoline. There is enough of it in the United States to literally burn the country down. Every gas station is a fueling depot for incendiaries, and there are gas stations on practically every corner in America.

Why Bombs and Incendiaries

It is pertinent to ask why the bombs and the incendiary, why these instruments in America when the classical weapons of revolution have been guns and bayonets. It was the gun and bayonet in China, in Cuba, and it is now in those Latin American countries where revolutionary movements are in process.

The bomb and incendiary are appropriate to America, of course, because our economy is characterized by a concentration of resources. We do not have cities lighted by ten thousand oil lamps, but by one central power generating plant. Almost every adult American has a car, and this is enabled by factory concentrations capable of economical production and gasoline-oil storage concentrations capable of providing a reliable supply of fuel. Our communications resources are concentrated in a few

Figure 1. Bomb damage, University of Wisconsin.

facilities; our transportation resources are concentrated along certain arterial pathways. Whatever end product we use in America, we can be reasonably sure that it was the subject of concentration at least once in its existence, i.e. during material acquisition, or processing-fabrication, or storage, or distribution.

Resource concentration has resulted in more material wealth for the majority of our citizens than is enjoyed by the people of any other country. Concentration, then, is the key to our economic well-being. It is also the most vulnerable physical feature of our national structure. One bomb can turn out all the lights in a city, interrupt communications channels over a wide area, or stop the flow of traffic in important transportation arteries. Given such circumstances, the revolutionary would be foolish to resort to the gun and bayonet. And given such circumstances, the revolutionary has an opportunity through organized, wide-scale bomb and incendiary attacks to strike devastating blows against the American system and the American people.

On the basis of the evidence (and knowledgeable projections of it) we can conclude that the threat, the intention, and the potential are real, ugly, and massive. This portends a continuing crisis of violence fashioned by people whose apparent objectives may be policial, but who also seem motivated by a psychopathic passion for destruction. The prospects translate into a particularly viscious threat to the free enterprise system and those organizations who are part of it.

TARGET SUSCEPTIBILITY

Recognizing the threat in general terms, we next need some insight into those attributes or characteristics which are typical of specific targets. This is a relative thing. As noted previously, every institution in the free enterprise system is potentially a target. But there are factors such as visibility, location, and social involvement which have played a part in making certain institutions objects of violence.

There currently is no effective organized direction of the revolutionary movement at the national level. Local conditions and local attitudes often are the forcing functions that select the target and determine the type and degree of violence. Sabotage and terrorism, the traditional objectives of the revolutionary, are indeed reflected in many of the incidents. But visible prominence in our national life is also an attribute that makes a target. This is evidenced by such incidents as the abortive Statue of Liberty plot, the Haymarket Square (Chicago) bombing, and the U.S. Capital bombing.

Large corporations have visible prominence, and this serves as a focus of violence. GM, IBM, Chase Manhattan, General Electric, Sears Roebuck, B of A and other corporate giants have all known the savage thrust of violence because they are big. What is true nationally is true locally. A company is also a potential target if, though not a national giant, it is highly prominent in its own community. A prominent issue also makes a company susceptible. It was napalm in the case of Dow; pollution, most probably, where oil companies have been involved. If a real issue emerges or an artificial one can be contrived, it will serve as the seed for an occasion of violence.

Prominence is, then, one criterion by which a company's susceptibility to bombing can be determined. Another is proximity to a center or a scene of radical activity. Bank of America's Isle Vista branch was a target of opportunity during a violent uprising spawned on the adjacent Santa Barbara campus. No one would have traveled from San Francisco to Santa Barbara specifically to destroy the Isle Vista facility, and were there no Bank of America branch at Isle Vista, none of the demonstrators would have gone to another city to seek a branch. It was a situation of mindless violence focusing on the most apparent target. Bombings and incendiary attacks in Kent, Ohio, and in the vicinity of Berkeley also represent violent outlets against the most convenient, the most available target.

Active involvement in social issues or political activities can make an organization or an individual a target. It matters not on which side of a question a stand is taken; there are extremists reflecting the opposite viewpoint who will create an event of violence. It is enough only that a stand be taken. The president of one of the largest telephone companies in the United States was killed by a bomb placed in his car because he stood up for his convictions, because he was genuinely concerned about economic repression of minorities and was trying to do something about it in the hiring policies of his company.

Where the social or political activity is person-oriented, i.e. is generated by a single prominent company executive, violent retaliation is usually restricted to the person involved and takes place in his home, car, or office. Where a company or institution as a whole generally represents a certain philosophical stance, violent retaliation will be directed against the property assets of the enterprise.

In summary, you and/or your organization are more susceptible to violence if you reflect national or local prominence, are located close to a center of extreme viewpoints, or are known to represent certain political or social philosophies. But even if you don't meet these criteria, you still could become a target. This is a possibility faced by every industry, business, and school in the United States today, and it poses a new challenge in terms of protecting personnel and property. However, with intelligence and prudent safeguards, we can establish a security capability for our institutions which is equal to the threat. The first step is to recognize the fact that the threat *is* ugly, and real, and massive.

II

THE TECHNOLOGY OF EXPLOSIVE
AND INCENDIARY VIOLENCE

THE average revolutionary spends more time rationalizing his violence than learning the practical art of it carefully and well. As a consequence, many of the devices used today reflect faulty design and shoddy craftsmanship. There is in this an elemental danger to the bomber, and a number of them bent on violence have fallen victim to their own amateurism. Bombers have been blowing themselves up with jarring regularity throughout the country (New York, Minneapolis, Compton, California, to name but a few locations), though for some sanguinary souls probably not frequently enough.

The faults and fatal defects that characterize these devices represent, in addition to the danger to the bomber, a considerable additional risk to others. A device may be planned as a time bomb with an alarm clock for the delay, but sloppy arrangement of lead wires or poor isolation of contact points may create a condition where it is possible to effectively close the circuit and fire the assembly accidentally by moving, shaking, or tipping the device.

This section on technology is designed to enable an understanding of this type of hazard as well as the hazard that is created as a result of normal bomb functioning. The material covers the operation and recognition characteristics of complete bombs and incendiaries and of the components that make up these assemblies. There is also a discussion of various employment techniques to provide a background for the protective measures that are discussed later.

EXPLOSIVE BOMBS

Explosives

An explosive, in the classical definition, is a chemical compound

14

which upon the application of heat, shock, or friction decomposes rapidly, liberating substantial amounts of energy. Explosives are generally classified into two groups: deflagrating or "low" explosives, those that normally react by burning, and detonating or "high" explosives, those that react by initiating and sustaining a true detonation wave. The difference between the two is best appreciated in terms of typical performance in reaction rates and maximum pressures.

	Low Explosive	*High Explosive*
Reaction Rate (Unconfined)	Burning Speed measured in seconds per inch/ft., in some cases feet per second	Detonating Speed measured in miles per second
Maximum pressure	Approx. 150,000 psi when fully confined	Detonation front pressure up to 4,000,000 psi (confinement not necessary)

While the classification (low explosive-high explosive) is generally valid in terms of the way explosives are traditionally employed, it should not be regarded as absolutely limiting. Some explosives normally categorized as low, for instance, will truly detonate if subjected to the proper stimulus, and most high explosives will burn, relatively slowly, without detonating. However, the classification does provide a convenient breakdown for visualizing explosives as they are normally used.

Low Explosives

Low explosives are most commonly employed as propellents and as ignition agents (as in time fuses, squibs, primers, and pyrotechnic assemblies). Sometimes, however, a low explosive is loaded into a fragmentation container and used as the main explosive charge. This type of application has virtually disappeared from military ordnance, but it has become a favorite, particularly in the form of the pipe bomb, of the revolutionary.

The speed with which a low explosive reacts depends on the degree to which it is confined. Low explosives in the open, as in a column on the ground, will burn slowly, though some, like black powder, burn much more rapidly than others. However, when these explosives are confined in a container, the rate of burning increases dramatically. The speed of the reaction is so fast that it does seem to be an instantaneous blast, a real detonation, even though it is still a burning process that the explosive undergoes. An excellent example is the small arms cartridge. When the propellent is ignited, it deflagrates instantly and generates such high pressures that the projectile is forced down the barrel at, in many cases, supersonic speeds. If this same powder is ignited in the open, however, it burns very slowly.

BLACK POWDER, the oldest explosive compound known to man, has also been the most durable. While a large number of explosive compounds have been developed since black powder, it is still commonly used today in such applications as ignition train elements and pyrotechnics. Black powder is simple to make, and the ingredients (potassium or sodium nitrate, 75%; charcoal, 15%; and sulfur, 10%) are readily available in most communities.

The explosive appears as small, irregularly shaped grains. Commercial black powder grains have shiny surfaces, which is the result of the graphite coating used to reduce friction in the mixing processes.

Black powder is a very unstable and sensitive explosive compound. It can be readily ignited by heat or friction, and once ignited, the flame front propagates through the mass very quickly.

SMALL ARMS PROPELLENTS. There are a number of small arms propellents that make effective fillers for low explosive bombs and that are readily available through commercial outlets. They are stocked by gun shops for the use of small arms buffs who do their own reloading. In quantities of 5 pounds or less, these low explosives do not come under the new Treasury Department regulations governing the storage, sale, and use of explosives. Some states do have laws governing the sale of less than 5 pounds of the propellents, but this is by no means universal. In many state jurisdictions, it is possible for almost anyone to buy propellent explosives without license, permit, or even identification.

If bulk smokeless powder is not available, small arms ammunition generally is, and this is another source of low explosives for bombs. There is enough powder in twenty-four shotgun shells to

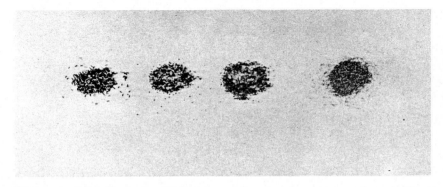

Figure 2. Propellents available at sporting goods stores make excellent explosives for fragmentation devices.

make a relatively small but very lethal fragmentation device.

Small arms propellents are normally much more stable and less sensitive than black powder. They usually appear as very small cylindrical or thin circular grains and may vary in color from shiny black to light brown.

High Explosives

High explosives do, as noted previously, truly detonate when subjected to a stimulus input sufficient in magnitude to start a detonation reaction. The responsiveness of an explosive to a stimulus input is known as its sensitivity. Some explosives are very sensitive to shock (as lead azide), while others (TNT, Explosive D) are very insensitive to it.

DYNAMITE. The most popular of commercial explosives and the one produced in the greatest quantity is dynamite. The term is practically generic since it now covers a wide variety of explosive compounds packed in the familiar brown paper-covered cartridge. The original dynamite consisted of nitroglycerine mixed into fesselguhr, an absorbent and itself inert powder. The fesselguhr desensitizes the highly volatile nitroglycerine to a degree enabling safe handling. In today's dynamites, the fesselguhr has been replaced by other desensitizers (except in Europe), such as wood fibers. Nitroglycerine is still used, but it is usually mixed with other ingredients, like ether glycol, to lower the freezing point or provide special blast or handling characteristics. Dynamites are normally relatively safe explosives but may deteriorate with age and become very sensitive.

Dynamite is readily recognizable because of its cylindrical, cartridge-like configuration and the brown or tan wrapper. These characteristics are typical whether the cartridge is 7/8 inch in diameter, 8 inches in length or 10 inches in diameter, 36 inches in length.

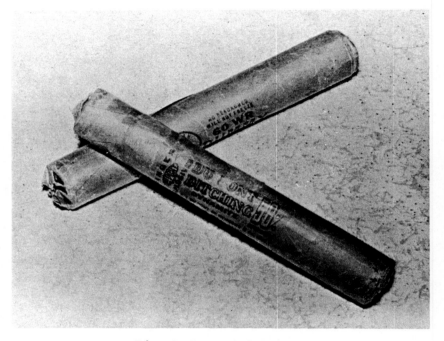

Figure 3. Commerical dynamite.

There are a number of other explosive compounds, such as blasting gelatins and ammonium nitrate mixtures, which are also packed in brown cartridge assemblies. Some of these are variations of dynamite, and each has functional characteristics which make it appropriate for certain types of blasting work. All of it, however, will function effectively in a bomb, although some, like Nitramon, are relatively insensitive and require special boostering.

NITROGLYCERIN. Most revolutionary texts on bombs and incendiaries describe how nitroglycerine can be made using sulfuric acid, nitric acid, and glycerin, or how it can be obtained from dynamite. Following these directions is a good way to end a revolutionary career. Nitro is one of the most dangerous explosive compounds to work with. Even when produced under precisely controlled laboratory conditions by experienced chemists, nitro does occasionally blow up. It is strictly not an explosive that is suitable for basement-type operations.

Revolutionaries seem to have recognized the dangers of nitro, for they have given it a wide berth. In some cases nitro has been reported, but on close examination the material was found to be some other liquid, usually harmless.

Nitroglycerin appears as a yellowish, viscous fluid. It is extremely sensitive to shock or heat. If encountered, it should be circumspectly avoided. The only persons competent to deal with it are chemists and bomb disposal technicians.

PLASTIC EXPLOSIVES. There are a number of plastic demolition compounds, most of which use the powerful explosive RDX as the base. Plastic refers to the pliability, the malleability of the explosive. In consistency very much like carpenter's putty, the explosive can be readily shaped to provide the best physical form for a specific demolition requirement. It can, for instance, be packed around a steel girder or be pressed into intimate contact with a masonry wall for maximum effectiveness.

Plastic explosives are not normally used commercially, primarily because they are so much more expensive than other explosives that will provide essentially the same result. But the plastics are stocked and employed extensively by the military. The particular attribute that makes them militarily desirable is their long-term stability in storage. They will not leak or settle under storage conditions as will some types of dynamite for instance, and the plastic explosives do not require special handling in extremely cold weather.

Plastic explosives used by revolutionaries, then, are most likely to be stolen military stocks. The military has two types of plastic explosives in use, C3 and C4. C3, the earlier formulation, is rapidly

disappearing from inventory, but it still is occasionally encountered. It is orangish-brown in color, crystalline in texture, and oily
to the touch. C4 is white in color and very much like putty in
texture.

Neither compound is sensitive to shock, heat, or friction. Both
can be safely handled using common sense safeguards; no
elaborate precautions are necessary.

The plastic explosives are not fantastic new compounds so
powerful that 1 cubic centimeter, for example, can level a
building. Journalistic sensationalism sometimes creates such fanci-
ful ideas, but they have little truth in hard reality. The plastics are
generally more powerful than dynamites, particularly in the area
of brisance or shattering power, but the increase in destructive
capability is definitely not at the magnitude level.

OTHER MILITARY EXPLOSIVES. The explosives used by the
military in such ordnance items as artillery projectiles, bombs,
grenades, and rockets constitute a long list. There is TNT, for
instance, and such TNT-based compounds as ammonal, amatol,
and PETN. There is tetryl, used primarily as a booster, and
Explosive D (Dunnite), which is employed in ordnance in which
the explosive must withstand extremely high impact forces
without detonating (as in armor piercing applications).

Though the military does have a wide variety of explosives for
use in munitions, the explosives are generally not available to the
revolutionary. There have been instances where explosive Comp. B
has been unloaded from Claymore mines in Viet Nam and has
been subsequently shipped back to the States for use in civil
violence, but cases like this have been relatively rare. The most
common sources of supply for high explosives have been and
remain commercial demolition supplies (bought or stolen), stolen
military demolitions, and ammonium nitrate fertilizer.

Blasting Accessories

Blasting Caps

Blasting caps are used to initiate high explosive charges. They
are made in a variety of sizes (strengths) and with such functional

Figure 4. Ammonium nitrate prills.

features as fractional second delays. All of them, however, are divided into two basic groups, electric and nonelectric, based on the type of energy used for activation. All of them, also, are manufactured as small cylindrical configurations with metal casings that are either aluminum or copper. The electric cap is larger (considering identical strength ratings) than the nonelectric cap and has, in addition, clearly recognizable lead wires extending from it.

Blasting caps are the most sensitive of commercially available high explosives items. They can be initiated by shock or heat and should therefore be handled with reasonable care.

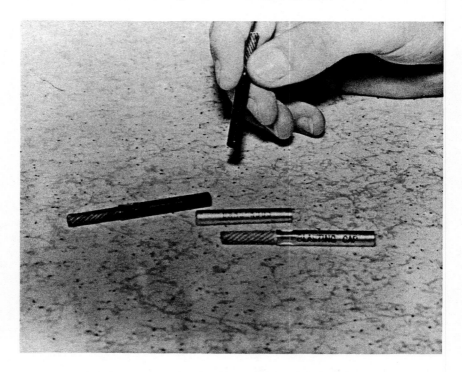

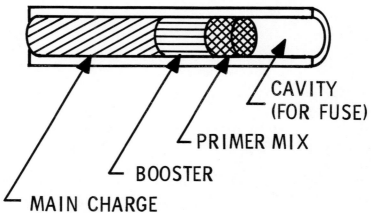

CAVITY
(FOR FUSE)

PRIMER MIX

BOOSTER

MAIN CHARGE

Figure 5. Blasting caps, nonelectric.

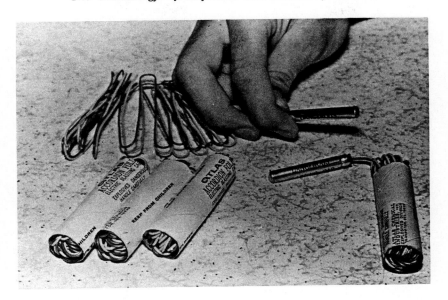

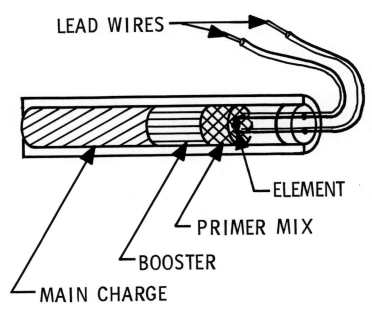

Figure 6. Blasting caps, electric.

Time Fuse

Time fuse consists of black powder tightly wrapped with several layers of fiber and waterproofing material and may be almost any color, black, white, green with orange being the most common. The fuse is used to initiate nonelectric blasting caps after a delay which is determined by the length and the burning rate. The most popular rate is 35 to 40 seconds per foot.

Time fuse is recognizable by the braided strand appearance, the solid color, and the black granular powder in the center. Fuse is not any significant hazard itself. It burns, of course, rather than detonates, but even in burning it is not dangerous except under unusual conditions.

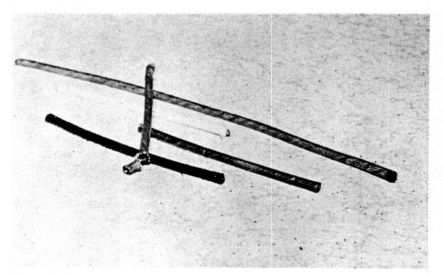

Figure 7. Time fuse is readily recognizable because of its solid exterior color and central core of black powder.

Detonating Cord

Most detonating cords consist of a high explosive column (usually PETN or a variation of it) wrapped in layers of cotton and rayon. In exterior appearance, detonating cord looks very much like time fuse in that it is stranded, about the same size, and similarly pliable. However, detonating cord is usually red or yellow and has a spiral strand of a contrasting color (green or black). Also, the explosive filler in the center is not black, as in fuse, but creamy to white.

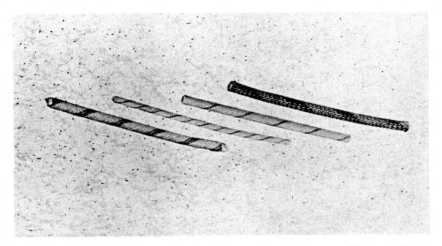

Figure 8. Most detonating cord has a solid background color (red or yellow) with a contrasting spiral (green, black) and a central core that is creamy to white.

Detonating cord is most commonly used to explosively connect demolition charges. It must be initiated with a blasting cap. It cannot be activated with a match or igniter as a fuse can. It is not particularly sensitive (is at least as safe as dynamite), but since it is a high explosive, reasonable care should be exercised in handling.

Firing Trains

In the traditional firing sequence, explosive initiation is started with a small amount of a relatively sensitive explosive and is passed on to increasingly less sensitive explosives. Where a low explosive is the main charge, all elements leading up to that main charge will be low explosives. For instance, in a low explosive-loaded hand grenade, there is, in functional sequence, a primer (activated by the striker), a pyrotechnic delay, an ignition element, and the main low explosive charge.

The primer converts a mechanical input into a thermal output, the delay provides time for the user to take safe cover after throwing the grenade, and the ignition unit amplifies the thermal impulse to ensure ignition of the main explosive charge. In a high explosive assembly, the original impetus may be thermal, with subsequent translation to detonation shock as other explosive compounds are encountered. Blasting caps, both electric and nonelectric, are typical of this initiation sequence. In a non-electric cap, the fuse supplies the initial thermal impulse. A heat-sensitive explosive translates this input into a detonation output, which initiates the next high explosive element in line. The electric cap uses a high resistance wire (which is in close proximity to a heat-sensitive low explosive) to start the initiation train. When current is dumped across the wire, the wire heats and ignites the low explosive. The thermal output of the low explosive initiates an adjacent high explosive which produces a detonation shock output.

In general, the explosive train is a series of explosive elements so arranged that the effect is amplified at each step, though some steps may perform other functions, such as time delays.

Initiating (Firing) Techniques

The initiating (or firing) technique refers to the means used to start the explosive train sequence. There are two basic initiating techniques, non-electric and electric.

In the nonelectric approach, some manual or mechanical means provides the initiation energy. It may be striking a match and applying the flame to a fuse, or it could be a firing pin impinging on a primer. Electrical energy may be used in the fuse somewhere (as a clock delay mechanism which activates a relay to which is attached a striker), but electrical energy doesn't directly initiate the first explosive element in line.

In electric initiation, electric energy does fire the first explosive element. An electric cap is usually employed, but the initiator may be a squib or even a photoflash bulb. Dumping electric current across the high resistance wire of the cap (or the squib or the filament of the photoflash) causes it to undergo an extremely fast

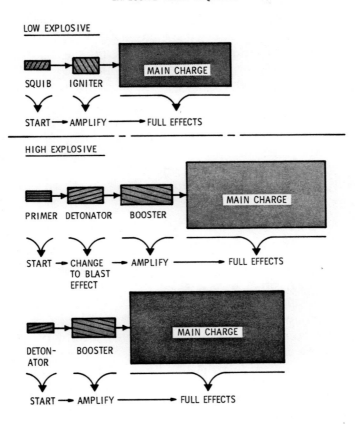

EXPLOSIVE TRAIN SEQUENCE

THE SEQUENCE ALWAYS STARTS WITH A SMALL AMOUNT OF SENSITIVE EXPLOSIVE AND PROGRESSES THROUGH AMPLIFICATION STAGES TO A COMPARITIVELY LARGE AMOUNT OF RELATIVELY INSENSITIVE EXPLOSIVE.

Figure 9

heat rise, and this initiates the adjacent explosive element.

In the electric circuit, there is an electric initiation device (cap, squib, or bulb), a power source (battery, hellbox, or line current), and a switch. The switch, which dumps current across the electric initiation device under the circumstances desired, can take many forms. An alarm clock can be a switch, as can a clothespin, or even a mousetrap, depending on the type of fuzing and the effects desired.

Bomb Fuzing

A fuze* is that element that applies the energy to initiate the bomb at the time and place desired. For bombs that are used passively (i.e. are planted or emplaced as compared to being · thrown), there are three basic fuzing techniques: time delay, target-activated, and remote controlled.

Time Delay Mechanisms

In the time delay mechanism, a fuze timing device (clockwork, chemical delay, time fuse) is activated, and the bomb explosive charge is automatically detonated when the delay period expires. This is the most popular type of bomb fuzing in use today. It enables the bomber to select a precise time for bomb detonation. Thus, he can set the mechanism to initiate when he thinks the circumstances will be just right and will allow him ample time to escape.

The simplest time delay device is achieved with time fuse and an explosive assembly. The fuse can be used to initiate a low explosive directly, or it may be assembled with a blasting cap to initiate a high explosive. In either case, the functioning is essentially the same. The bomber ignites the fuse, the fuse burns slowly along its length and, when the fire front reaches the far end, emits a spit of flame. The flame initiates the low explosive or the detonator. The time delay, of course, is dependent on the length of the fuse.

---

*Distinguished from fuse, which, as previously is a cord containing black powder and is used to provide time delay in nonelectric firing.

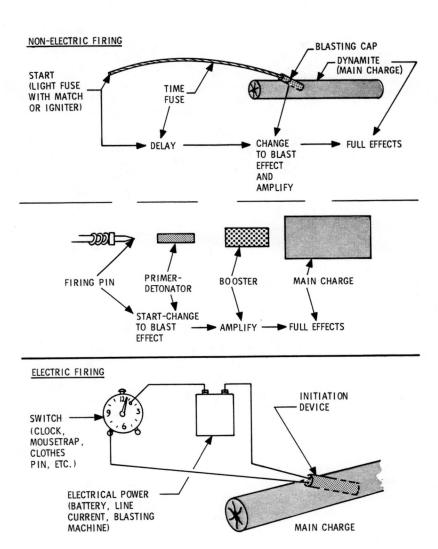

NON-ELECTRIC FIRING

BLASTING CAP

DYNAMITE
(MAIN CHARGE)

START
(LIGHT FUSE
WITH MATCH
OR IGNITER)

TIME
FUSE

START → DELAY → CHANGE TO BLAST EFFECT AND AMPLIFY → FULL EFFECTS

FIRING PIN

PRIMER-DETONATOR

BOOSTER

MAIN CHARGE

START-CHANGE TO BLAST EFFECT → AMPLIFY → FULL EFFECTS

ELECTRIC FIRING

SWITCH
(CLOCK,
MOUSETRAP,
CLOTHES
PIN, ETC.)

INITIATION
DEVICE

ELECTRICAL POWER
(BATTERY, LINE
CURRENT, BLASTING
MACHINE)

MAIN CHARGE

Figure 10

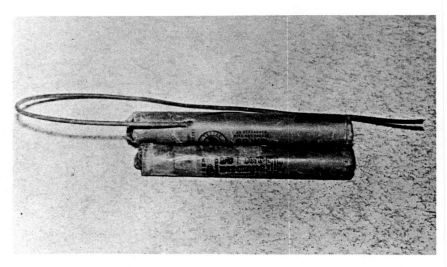

Figure 11. The simplest high explosive bomb consists of time fuse, a nonelectric cap, and the high explosive charge.

Time delay mechanisms with time fuse are cheap, safe, and reliable. However, time fuse has functional characteristics which limit its usefulness under certain conditions. Time fuse produces smoke in burning, and the smoke is characterized by a particularly acrid odor. In the confines of a building, a time fuse device would probably be detected quickly, maybe even before the bomber made his escape. In addition, it is not practicable to achieve long delays (hours) with time fuse.

If the bomber wants to penetrate a building or to achieve relatively long delays, he will usually use a delay mechanism other than time fuse. He has an infinite variety of techniques from which to choose, using mechanical, electrical, or chemical approaches.

MECHANICAL DELAYS. The most popular mechanical technique is the clockwork mechanism. Clockwork devices are cheap and reliable, and it requires no sophisticated expertise to rig an effective clockwork delay using either an alarm clock or a watch. If size is not a consideration, an alarm clock is usually selected since it is normally cheaper and is easier to work with. In some cases, one of the circuit lead wires is attached to the body of the clock, and the other lead is attached to a point on the face of the clock where it will intersect the hour hand. When the hour hand has rotated to the point where it contacts the projecting lead, the circuit is effectively closed (the entire clock assembly through the hour hand acts as one leg of the circuit) and the device fires. In at least one case, the bomber used a clock with plastic hands, and the device, of course, did not function.

Figure 12. The ready availability of alarm clocks and the relative ease with which they can be turned into timing switches makes them ideal for suitcase bombs.

Another clock technique is to use the winding stem of the alarm side to close the circuit. The winding stem rotates when the alarm goes off, and this movement is readily adaptable to a switch closure. In some cases, the winding stem approach can be used with no modification to the clock whatsoever. This depends, of course, on the mechanical makeup of the clock itself.

Most of the alarm clock delays employed by the FLQ in Canada feature winding stem switches. The FLQ devices are carefully crafted with soldered circuit connections and epoxied and insulated standoff contacts. By contrast, the American variety reflects a low level of workmanship with haphazard connections and poorly assembled electrical standoffs.

When the bomb assembly is too small to easily accommodate an alarm clock (as a pipe bomb or cigar box package), a wrist watch can be utilized. Some slight modifications are required, but it is neither difficult nor time consuming. The watch crystal is removed, and the second hand is taken off. If the delay desired is up to 60 minutes, the hour hand is removed; and if the delay is in hours (up to 12), the minute hand is removed. Then the crystal is replaced and a small screw is tapped through it at a location enabling the hand, on its rotation around the face, to contact the screw. Finally, one circuit lead is attached to the body of the watch, the other to the screw. When the hand subsequently moves around and touches the screw, the circuit closes and the device fires.

Clocks and watches are the most popular mechanical delays, but new and equally effective approaches are turning up all the time. One is the ice cube delay, assembled with a cube of ice holding a spring-loaded switch of some kind (usually a hacksaw blade) out of contact. As the ice melts, the contact arm moves closer to the contact point until contact is eventually made, firing the device. An ice cube used with a hacksaw blade will provide a delay of 45 minutes to one hour in a 70°F environment. In the summertime, it may indeed require some logistic planning on the part of the bomber to transport an ice cube to the bomb plant location without significant melting, but bombers in the past have shown great ingenuity in such things, and the ice cube approach is very cheap.

Another inexpensive time delay mechanism is the dried bean (or rice or pea) fuze. When placed in water, dried beans swell, more than doubling their volume, and this is a time-related phenomenon that can be used to delay the firing of a device. The beans are placed in the bottom of a jar, and a metal plate is placed on top of them. Two contact members are run through the lid and extended downward so that they face, but are separated from, the plate.

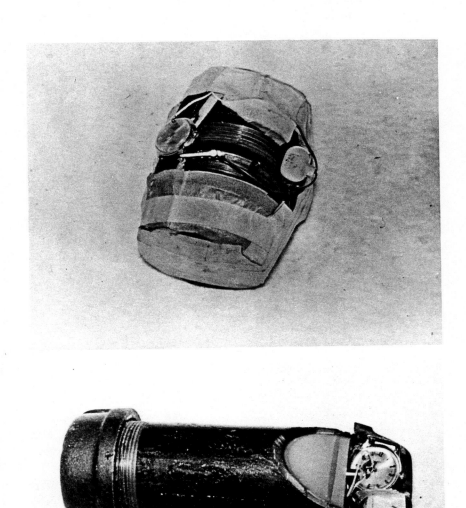

Figure 13. In the upper photo, a wristwatch timing device is secured to the outside of the bomb. The wristwatch can, however, be completely enclosed in a small bomb assemble as shown in the cutaway model, bottom photo.

The delay is initiated by pouring water into the jar until the beans are covered. The beans then swell and force the plate upward until it touches the two contact points and completes the circuit to fire the device. With this technique, a delay of up to 3 hours can be readily achieved using the family size mayonnaise jar.

ELECTRICAL DELAYS. Electrical delays can be obtained through a great variety of techniques. A simple approach, for instance, is to take a battery-operated relay, set it up so that relay closure completes the circuit, then energize it with a battery to hold the circuit open. Eventually, the battery will drain down below the threshold required to keep the relay open, and it will close and fire the device. An operational bonus achieved by the bomber in this type of device is that should someone seek to disarm the bomb by cutting a battery lead, the relay will, of course, close and initiate the firing train. It has, then, a built-in antidefeat mechanism.

Target-activated Devices

Target-activated devices are those that are initiated by a stimulus input of some kind provided by the target itself. Usually the target is a human being, and in doing some normal, predictable act he unwittingly supplies the type and level of energy required to activate the killing mechanism. When a human is the target, the technique is known as the booby trap. Target-activated devices can also be used to damage or destroy trains, aircrafts, ships, and even buildings by utilizing some energy output that they characteristically produce.

In homemade bombs used against humans, electrically fired devices are preferred, and the action of the target results in switch closure to fire the device. Very simple household hardware can be used for the switch. A popular technique is to use a spring clothespin. Electrical points are incorporated into the two inner contact surfaces of the clothespin and connected by lead wires to the firing circuit. When the clothespin is closed, the contact points touch to complete the circuit. A small wooden wedge placed inside the clothespin jaws keeps the contacts apart, and a cord secured to the wedge and tied to something the target will move

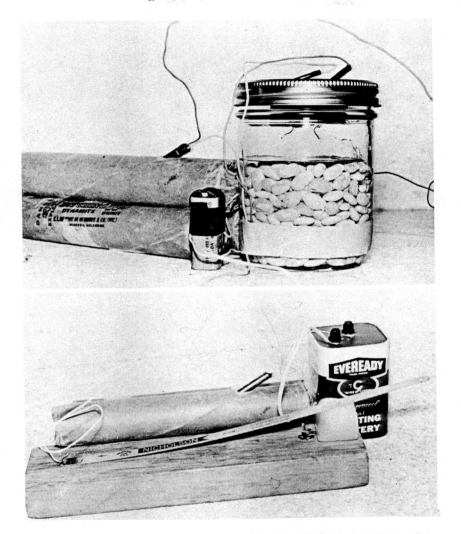

Figure 14. Bean delay fuze. When the water-soaked beans expand, they force the plate upward. The circuit is closed and the assembly fires when the plate touches the two exposed contact wires.

Figure 15. Ice cube delay. When the ice melts, the hacksaw blade will touch the contact point and complete the circuit to fire the device.

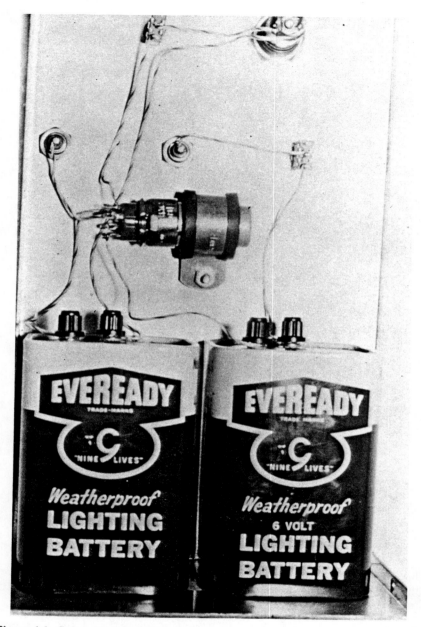

Figure 16. Solenoid delay. The solenoid (center) is held in the open position by one of the batteries. When the current output of the battery falls below the threshold required to keep the solenoid open, it closes and completes the circuit for the other battery to fire the device.

completes the triggering mechanism. Were the cord tied to a doorknob, the wedge would be pulled out of the clothespin to activate the bomb when the target opened the door.

A mousetrap can be used as a switch in a number of ways. With the spring held in the cocked position by the top of a box, opening the lid will release the spring and allow it to snap over to the reverse side of the wooden base. By putting an electrical contact at this point and using the spring itself as part of the circuit, the mousetrap becomes an effective switch.

The mousetrap can also be used (as the clothespin) with a wedge under the spring and the wedge tied to something the target will move. When he does, the wedge is pulled from under the spring which then snaps down to close the circuit and fire the device.

Antidisturbance switches represent a technological escalation in target-activated fuzing. The switch is designed to close and function the bomb when the explosive mechanism is moved. In a package assembly, the antidisturbance feature activates if the package is picked up, tilted, or turned. It is not difficult to make a switch so sensitive that it will activate even if the basic assembly is just barely touched.

The simplest of hardware can be used for antidisturbance switches. A small bell, for instance, can easily be modified to function as an antidisturbance mechanism. The clapper is removed and replaced with a weighted circuit member suspended from the clapper hook by string or insulated wire. The modified clapper then becomes one part of the circuit, the bell body itself the other, and when contact is made between them, there is in effect a switch closure.

Mercury switches make good antidisturbance mechanisms as revolutionary literature is quick to point out. A mercury mechanism may be procured from a silent light switch and modified for an antidisturbance device, or the entire light switch may be used for a fuzing mechanism that is orientation dependent. The bomber rigs it into some kind of package assembly that is planted so that the target is tempted to turn it over, as, for instance, a radio that is placed upside down on a table.

Setting up the target-activated bomb in the victim's car is a

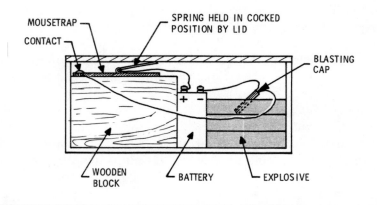

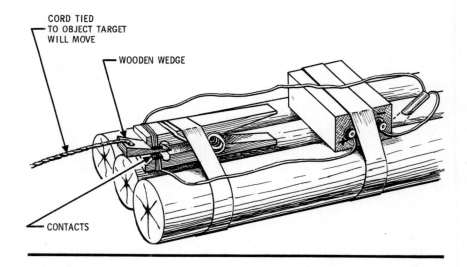

MOUSETRAP FUZING DEVICE (TOP)

CLOTHESPIN FUZING DEVICE (BOTTOM)

Figure 17

favored technique. A car is usually accessible at one time or another under conditions enabling the bomber to work covertly in installing a device. In addition, it contains its own power source and has a wonderful variety of physical phenomena (acceleration, deceleration, centrifugal force, heat, and windstream among others) and switches (ignition, lights, heater, radio) which can be used to trigger a device.

Most car bombs are rigged, however, directly across the ignition switch. This is very easy to do, and it can be done very quickly. One electrical lead is attached to the hot side of the coil, the other to body ground. With a little practice, the device can be emplaced and connected in less than a minute. When the target turns the ignition key, battery power flows to the detonator and the bomb explodes.

Remote-controlled

The remote-controlled device is one that is activated by the user while he is located at a position remote from the bomb. The bomber may be several blocks or several miles away when he initiates the device through some sort of technique like a radio signal. Thus, he is able to control the exact time of the detonation, even delay it from the original plan if he desires, and still remain safely removed from the effects.

The revolutionary in America has not as yet used remote-controlled devices, although they are relatively easy to make and they do have obvious tactical advantages. It can reasonably be expected that as the political extremists become more expert through experimentation and experience, they will add the remote-controlled bomb to their repertory of violence.

But though the revolutionaries have not as yet used it, criminals have, and two recent cases serve to illustrate the basic technology. In one case, the device which used two pipe bombs was assembled with the basic components of a remote-controlled model airplane kit. The pipe bombs were strapped together between two pieces of balsa wood; the radio-receiving elements were mounted on the top and the motor on the bottom piece of balsa. Three kitchen matches were epoxied to the propeller shaft of the motor. The

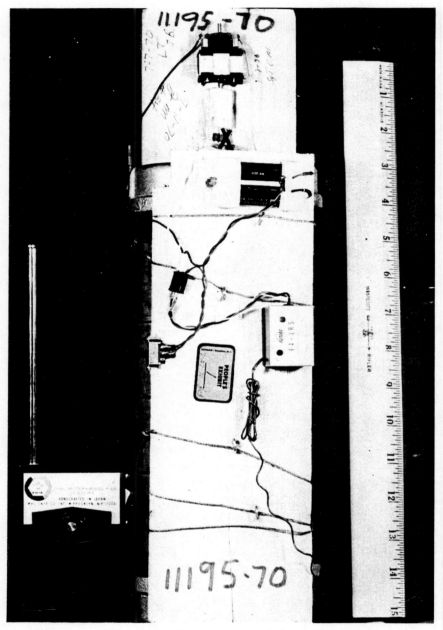

Figure 18. Remote-controlled bomb recovered by police in suburb of large city.

matchheads rested against emery paper, and two lengths of quickmatch positioned above the matches led into the low explosive-filled pipe bomb.

To activate the device, the bomber would merely transmit a signal from the remote control unit. The receiver element on the bomb would pick up the transmission and automatically apply battery power to the motor. As the motor would turn up, the matches would grind into the emery board, burst into flame, and ignite the two pieces of quickmatch. The flame front would then be conveyed by the quickmatch into the two bombs, resulting in ignition of the main explosive charges.

In this case, the bomber had apparently intended to use the device to murder a relative. He was apprehended by the police before he could put his plan into practice. In an examination of the device, police bomb disposal specialists found that it was a particularly lethal instrument. The low explosive, similar to that used in cherry bombs, was very energetic. The police also found that the receiving element would respond to signals from various other types of equipment, such as portable radios.

In another case, a bomber used a remote-controlled assembly to hold up a bank. The device contained in a package was placed in the drawer of a drive-in window. Written instructions with the package informed the teller that it was a bomb and that it would be detonated unless all immediately available cash was returned in the drawer. The teller shelled out about two thousand dollars, and the bomber drove away. Bomb squad technicians subsequently determined the device to be an artillery simulator used by the military, not a very powerful instrument but one certainly capable of destroying a person's vision or inflicting other serious injury.

MAIN CHARGE ASSEMBLIES. The main charge is the bulk of the explosive material used in a bomb, and it directly produces practically all of the destruction. There are two kinds of effects normally desired: straight blast for physical damage and blast plus fragmentation for killing. Blast is very effective in destroying things, and it will kill if the victim is close enough to the device. To ensure death where the victim may not be right next to the bomb when it explodes, a fragmentation envelope of some kind around the explosive is used.

One approach is to secure fragmentation hardware (nails, nuts and bolts, tacks, staples) to the outside of the explosive. When the explosive detonates, this material will be torn into small fragments and propelled outward at velocities that may range from 3000 to 5000 feet per second, depending on the type of explosive employed. At that speed, these jagged fragments will rip and tear through flesh and bone with slashing savagery.

The reverse approach is to put the explosive inside a metal container (pipe, tool box) that itself will break up under blast effects and provide good fragmentation, and this is the most popular fragmentation approach today, with the pipe bomb the most widely used configuration. It is a favorite of the revolutionary because, besides being effective, it has symbolic significance as a true weapon of the people. It is also easy to assemble. A child can make one. Children do; in fact, twelve-year-olds in New York City.

Blast bomb (no fragmentation) assemblies come in a variety of forms. If the bomber feels he must conceal the device, it is normally packaged in a briefcase or travelling bag. Either one provides him an easily carried assembly that is perfectly innocent and innocuous in most environments. If concealment is not a concern to the bomber, he may make no attempt to disguise the bomb, and it may be encountered as a clearly visible explosive assembly with an attached fuze.

Disguised booby trap devices are rarely used today. The revolutionary is just not incorporating explosive assemblies into books, lamps, fountain pens, or telephones. There have been reports of booby-trapped cigarette lighters, but not many; and the devices documented were so poorly constructed as to be practically nonhazardous. The closest thing to a disguised device in any quantity has been the explosive assembly contained in the mailed package. Mailed packages, however, have been relatively rare in the current bombing wave.

INCENDIARY DEVICES

The functioning of an incendiary device follows the same sequential logic as that of an explosive instrument. There is either

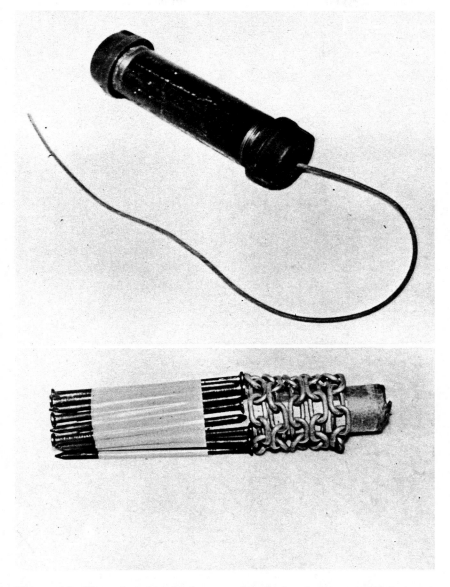

Figure 19. The pipe bomb (upper photo) is the most widely used fragmentation device. However, other fragmentation assemblies using chains or nails wrapped around the explosive (lower photo) have been found.

an electrical or nonelectrical initiation of some kind, and there is then a series (or train) of elements, each of which amplifies the effect until the main incendiary charge has been initiated.

Molotov Cocktail

The Molotov cocktail has the simplest of series elements. The main incendiary charge (usually a mixture of gasoline and fuel oil) is contained in a bottle. A rag stuffed into the opening draws out some of the inflammable liquid and serves as a wick. The wick is ignited just before the Molotov is thrown; and when the bottle hits and breaks, the gas-fuel oil mixture spills out and is ignited.

A currently popular variation on the Molotov is to add sulphuric acid to the gasoline in a bottle, then apply a mixture of potassium chlorate and sugar to a rag wrapped around the bottle. When it is thrown and breaks, the constituents ignite spontaneously. This is a handy approach since it is not necessary to take time to light the wick before the device can be thrown.

Figure 20. *Left.* Typical Molotov cocktail. *Right.* Potassium chlorate and sugar are contained in the small bottle and sulfuric acid and gasoline are mixed in the large bottle. The chlorate-sugar is poured over the cloth binding just before the incendiary is thrown, and when it hits and breaks, the ingredients mix and ignite spontaneously.

INCENDIARY BOOBY TRAP

DEVICE, WHICH VERY CLEARLY RESEMBLES MOLOTOV COCKTAIL, IS
LEFT IN OBVIOUS LOCATION. SHOULD SOMEONE PICK IT UP, THE
LIQUID SLOSHES AGAINST THE ZINC WASHER AND HYDROGEN GAS
STARTS FORMING. EVENTUALLY GAS PRESSURE WILL RUPTURE THE
BOTTLE, AND THE SULPHURIC ACID WILL MAKE CONTACT WITH THE
POTASSIUM CHLORATE-SUGAR AND IGNITE SPONTANEOUSLY.

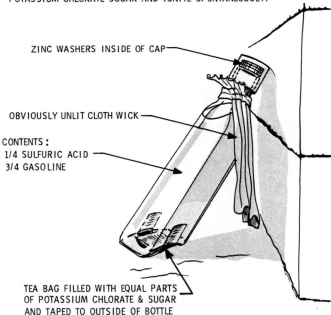

ZINC WASHERS INSIDE OF CAP

OBVIOUSLY UNLIT CLOTH WICK

CONTENTS :
1/4 SULFURIC ACID
3/4 GASOLINE

TEA BAG FILLED WITH EQUAL PARTS
OF POTASSIUM CHLORATE & SUGAR
AND TAPED TO OUTSIDE OF BOTTLE

Figure 21

Potassium Chlorate Incendiary

The potassium cholorate-sulphuricacid mixture approach is used in an incendiary device originally developed apparently to provide addicts a means of quickly destroying dope if apprehended. The device consists of two clam-like halves that open up to reveal a central cavity where the dope is stored. The halves are made of potassium chlorate and fiberglass resin, and embedded in one half is a glass vial of sulphuric acid that can be broken by pushing a wooden plunger that rests against the vial and extends to the outside of the container. When the vial is broken, spontaneous ignition occurs and the dope inside (plus the case itself) is entirely destroyed.

Revolutionaries have shown an interest in using this device for incendiary purposes, and it certainly has the potential. When ignited, the assembly burns with such fierce heat that the brass hinges melt. One of the proposed tactics is to hand it to a police officer, telling him as you do that it is something you just found. As he grasps it, you push the wooden plunger, and the assembly ignites and literally melts away his hand. It has not been possible to document a case in which a device was so used, but the proposal shows how deep and irrational is the hate that motivates acts of violence today.

Time Delay Incendiaries

Time delay fuzing is used infrequently in incendiaries, primarily because the incendiary as a weapon is more often used actively (in riots, insurrections, civil disorders) than passively. For those cases where incendiaries have been used passively, the cigarette delay, an old trick of arsonists, has sometimes been employed. Clock delay mechanisms have also been encountered, some using wristwatches in assemblies as small as a cigarette pack. There have been brief rashes of fire bombings using such incendiary instruments. About thirty of the devices were planted in one New York department store alone. However, the attacks have not been sustained, probably because since each incendiary unit requires a wristwatch, it is a relatively expensive way to start fires.

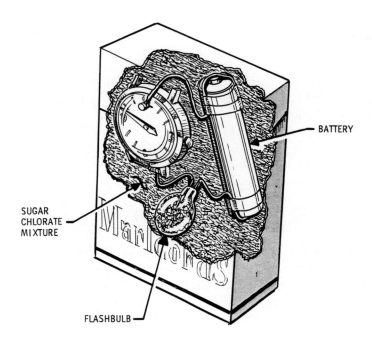

BATTERY

SUGAR
CHLORATE
MIXTURE

FLASHBULB

CIGARETTE PACK TIME DELAY INCENDIARY

Figure 22

Other Incendiary Techniques

Creating incendiary violence is easier than generating explosive violence. All you need, after all, is but a match. A match and gasoline were the only things used in destroying a Kroeger's market in Madison, Wisconsin. The rioters chopped a hole in the roof, poured in the gasoline, lighted a gas-soaked rag, and dropped it inside.

There are a number of commercial products which, because of functional characteristics, lend themselves naturally to use as incendiaries. Railroad fuses, now sold to motorists for highway emergency warning flares, are natural incendiary devices. They burn with a high heat and have an extended burning time. The hand-held sparkler, so familiar as part of traditional Fourth of July pyrotechnics, also makes a good incendiary under the right circumstances. In addition, an incendiary unit sold for fire fighting (used to create backfires) is ideal as an incendiary weapon in guerilla or insurrectionist activities.

EMPLOYMENT TECHNIQUES AND DESTRUCTIVE CAPABILITIES

No two bombings are exactly alike, as indeed, no two bombers or set of target circumstances are ever identical. Each incident forges its own uniqueness out of the individual characteristics of the device itself, how it is deployed, and the prevailing target circumstances. In an examination of the incidents of the past, however, there does emerge a set of patterns on employment techniques that can be useful in defining security measures. It is possible to determine, for instance, where most probably a bomb will be placed inside a building and what, on the basis of the historical record, its maximum size and destructive potential will be. This information then becomes helpful in determining in advance appropriate protective controls and in instituting effective reaction steps (search, evacuation) in a bomb situation.

Man-carried Explosive Bombs

The greatest extent of potential damage in a bomb incident is, obviously, a function primarily of the amount of explosives involved. If a bomber penetrates a building, the explosive charge will be limited to what he can conveniently carry; 25 pounds is about the maximum. Heavier charges than this have been carried into buildings, but infrequently; in most cases, the explosive charge has been less than 25 pounds.

The damage potential of 25 pounds of explosive is appreciable. This is not a very precise assessment, certainly, but greater precision can be wrought only out of a consideration of the specific circumstances. A 25-pound charge is not enough to bring a modern skyscraper tumbling to the ground, but it will, if well placed, do severe structural damage. Depending on venting, location, and building structural characteristics, it can exert a damage field encompassing the area two floors above and two floors below the floor on which it is placed. If the structure is small and light (frame wood or light sheet metal), 25 pounds can literally vaporize it.

As the amount of explosive is reduced, the damage radius is correspondingly decreased. By the time the explosive charge has been scaled down to one pound, the blast damage radius will essentially be confined to a single room (considering the charge to be placed on a table in the center of a 30 X 30 foot square room with masonry walls and reinforced floor and ceiling). In pipe bombs with a one pound, high explosive charge, there is potential for fragmentation travel outside the room; if a low explosive is used, particularly one of the less efficient low explosive compounds, fragmentation will at most invariably be contained within the room even though the walls are of thin, wooden construction.

In man-carried bombs placed outside of buildings, the practical weight limit is about 40 pounds. Damage will, of course, depend on where the bomb is placed in relation to primary building structure. If the device is close to or has physical contact with the building itself, the results can be devastating. Even if the assembly is slightly separated from the building, the difference (as compared to direct contact) in damage can be substantial. The distance-damage ratio is an inverse of the square foot function, and even an inch can be a significant factor.

If a device is placed outside a building, it will usually be hidden in a window well, behind shrubbery, at a junction point in the building, in a basement entranceway, or on the roof. The roof is frequently employed whether the device be explosive or incendiary. The key, of course, is concealment; the bomber will not normally place a device at an exterior building location where it is immediately visible.

When the bomber penetrates a building, he traditionally seeks a place of public access and personal privacy, i.e. any place he can get to without suspicion, and, once arrived, where he will be relatively alone. Predictably, then, the most popular place to plant a bomb is a public lavatory. Again and again, case records point up the frequency with which bombers seek out the rest rooms. In the bombing at Dayton's department store, Minnesota, Bluefield State College, Bluefield, Virginia, and the Cambridge County Courthouse in Maryland, the explosive assemblies were planted in rest rooms.

The next favored spot is a machinery or maintenance area of a building, although increasing security steps by building proprieters and managers to deny public access to these locations is forcing a change in this situation. If, however, a bomber can get to this type of location, he will use it for planting his charge. The bomb that wrecked the Des Moines Chamber of Commerce was placed in the basement boiler room.

Stairwells are the next most preferred location, and this may seem odd until you consider the pattern of pedestrian traffic flow in a modern building serviced by escalators and elevators. Even though the building is jammed, as a department store during the Christmas rush, traffic on the stairs is practically nonexistent. If you go to the

Figure 23. Clockwork bomb assemble removed from washroom of large city store.

Figure 24. Bomb damage to basement of Chamber of Commerce Building, Des Moines, Iowa.

stairwell of a modern building, you are almost invariably alone. It does provide the bomber a place of public access and personal privacy. The bomb in the Portugese Embassy in New York was placed on the stairwell.

In further declining order of preference, hallways, reception areas, and foyers are the next most popular. While these places are normally characterized by public access, they offer less in the way of public privacy than the locations previously listed. Still they are used; the bomb in the Los Angeles Times Building was placed in the reception area, the one used against GM in New York was located in a hallway.

The most unlikely area for a bomb to be planted is in the working spaces of a building, i.e. the office areas or assembly line floor. The reason is obvious. In such an area, the bomber would be recognized immediately as a stranger and could very well be questioned, the very last thing he would want.

The Mobile Bomb

On February 13, 1970, a night patrolman passing by the Canadian National Bank in Montreal late in the evening saw an old pink Volkswagon parked up against the bank building. Cars are not usually left overnight in this area (the appearance of one naturally then excited suspicion or, at least, curiosity), and it had the battered and forlorn look common to cars that are abandoned on city streets. The patrolman went to investigate more closely. What he saw sent him galloping to the nearest phone to place a call to the Montreal Bomb Squad.

There were 165 pounds of dynamite in the car, in the front seat, the back, and even in the trunk, and the whole thing was rigged as a bomb, as the Montreal Squad found out, with an alarm clock as the triggering mechanism. The alarm clock-battery circuit to the blasting cap was located next to the door adjacent to the building. The car was so close to the bank that the door on that side couldn't be opened, and the squad technicians had to go through the other door and work over the pile of dynamite to reach the fuze. It was hardly an ideal working environment. But they aborted the clock mechanism in time, actually with a comfortable margin of 25 minutes to spare, and spoiled a piece of conspicuous violence in the making.

It would, in fact, have been monumental violence. With the explosive charge placed that close to the building, damage significantly in excess of one million dollars was a clear possibility.

The use of a vehicle to transport and place an explosive assembly resulting in a mobile bomb is not new. The technique was employed in Algeria and Viet Nam. The Montreal incident, however, marked the first time this approach was utilized in the Northern Americas. The implications were sinister, and it was not long before the seed of the idea blossomed into fiery violence in the United States.

On the night of August 24, 1970, a truck was driven into an alley and parked next to the Army Research Center at the University of Wisconsin. Less than 20 minutes later, the sky above Madison, Wisconsin, lit up with a pyrotechnic glow, and a deafening roar rumbled through the town. For the truck was a mobile bomb containing 1700 pounds of explosive-processed ammonium nitrate fertilizer. One person was killed, several were injured, and property damage of approximately 6.5 million dollars was sustained. Revolutionary violence was coming to America on a colossal scale.

In another case, a group of political dissidents planned to place and detonate a mobile bomb containing 100 pounds of dynamite in front of the home of a chief of police. The explosive was obtained, and material for a fuzing mechanism was procured. At that time, the police, who through the agency of an informant had been following the unfolding conspiracy very closely, moved in and scotched the plot. Violence was averted in this particular instance, but because of the nature of the evidence and the manner in which it was assembled, the police did not have a case that would stand up in court. The conspirators were free to try again.

All of this points up the fact that the mobile bomb is a technique that we can expect to see used in the future. It is simple in concept, not difficult to assemble, and, of course, has a potential for vast destruction. That last, particularly, holds great appeal for the revolutionary.

III

PROTECTIVE MEASURES

No one can prescribe a single level and standard of protection that is uniformly appropriate for every business and industrial institution. Each enterprise is unique in terms of its physical layout, its personnel complement, and the degree to which it is a likely target for violence. Its protective capability must therefore be specifically structured to meet its own unique requirements. The protective measures discussed in this section are, then, general guidelines to be adopted with such modifications as are appropriate for individual circumstances.

The objective of protective measures is to deter the bomber or discourage or dissuade him to the extent that he abandons his plan of violence. If he doesn't abandon it altogether, he is at least forced to elect an alternative action yielding a lower level of destruction than he had originally contemplated, as in the case of a bomber who, convinced that protective measures are so tight that he can't penetrate a building, plants his bomb on the outside.

RESOURCE INVENTORY

Determining an appropriate set of protective safeguards begins with an inventory of the institutional resources requiring protection. The basic categories to be considered are resources representing
1. critical elements in company operations
2. substantial monetary value
3. energy sources capable of amplifying bomb effects (as a propane storage tank)
4. unique proprietary assets.
When these resources, which constitute potential targets, have been determined, they should be listed in a priority sequence. The scheme for issuing priority will depend very substantially on the type of institutional operation. The central switchboard of a

telephone company, for instance, would be a higher priority resource than would be the company's repair truck fleet.

The priority list becomes a valuable guideline in defining an appropriate protective plan for both exterior and interior areas. Those resources that are higher on the list should be given more security attention than thost further down on the list. The priority rankings also help to establish a sequence and a relative emphasis for a search plan.

PHYSICAL LAYOUT

The physical layout of a building or plant complex is a significant factor in deterring the bomb threat. Unfortunately, this aspect of security is not usually considered in the original layout design, and achieving effective deterrence frequently becomes a matter of modifying existing layouts to enhance the deterrent capability. Even though this is not the ideal situation, significant improvement in deterrent effectiveness can often be made through very simple and inexpensive modifications to an existing layout.

Exterior Areas

If the facility is adjoined by open premises (as a parking lot or equipment storage area) a barbed wire-topped cyclone fence integrated with good lighting around the entire perimeter will provide an effective deterrent. This will not be sufficient to stop a skilled saboteur, but it will certainly slow him up (increasing the possibility of detection), and it will definitely dissuade the amateur.

If it is a decision between lighting and fencing, lighting is preferable by far. The superiority of lighting in terms of deterrent capability has been proved innumerable times in actual use. Our experience in Viet Nam has demonstrated in countless cases that, when adequate perimeter lighting was installed around a base, the incidence of enemy penetrations and of intrusions by pilferers dropped dramatically. This deterrent effect is also evident in the results seen when lighting was installed or increased around public and private buildings in the United States.

Fencing without lighting is next to useless. It conveniently demarcates a proprietary boundary, but it deters hardly anyone. This is illustrated by the incident of the midwestern police department that was blown up by a bomb placed in an exterior window well. The official reaction was positive and swift — a chain link fence was erected around the entire building immediately. But no attention was given to lighting improvements nor to the many trees and bushes adjacent to the building that provided convenient cover for a covert approach. The predictable result: the station was bombed again and in almost the same place.

Perimeter fencing, to be fully effective, necessitates controlled access. The number of entrances should be limited to those required for expeditious work flow. Whether a gate is to be manned by a guard depends on the criticality of the resource stored within the enclosed area. If guards are necessary, access points can often be so located as to enable one guard to cover two accesses effectively.

The likelihood of bomb or incendiary loss can be reduced (and the probability of pilfering can be minimized also) by knowledge-able placement of stored material within a fenced enclosure. If possible, a standoff distance of at least 20 feet should be established between the fence and stored supplies. This provides a lane for vehicle or foot guard patrol and increases the difficulty of external access to the material.

Regardless of whether the supplies are stored immediately adjacent to the fence, the material should be arranged so that items that are expensive, critical, or inflammable are located in the center of the storage area in a place where they will be under increased surveillance, such as next to a manned gate.

Parking

With the advent of the mobile bomb, vehicle parking has become a critical security problem. The potential threat to facilities and installations is so apparent it does not need elaboration. It would be desirable to maintain a 300-foot, vehicle-free zone around every building, but this is not practicable in most circumstances. However, where the facility, installation, or

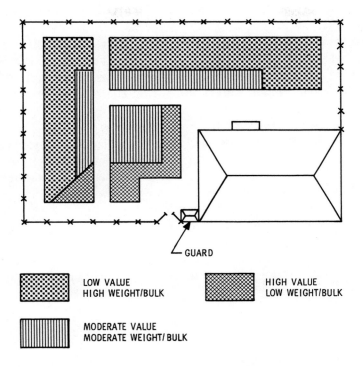

LOW VALUE
HIGH WEIGHT/BULK

HIGH VALUE
LOW WEIGHT/BULK

MODERATE VALUE
MODERATE WEIGHT/ BULK

THIS ARRANGEMENT PLACES THE LEAST VALUABLE MATERIEL IN THE
MOST VULNERABLE LOCATIONS. IT HELPS REDUCE LOSSES DUE TO
AN EXPLOSIVE OR INCENDIARY ATTACK, OR TO THEFT OR PILFERAGE.

OUTDOOR STORAGE LAYOUT

Figure 25

building represents a high priority target such as a fuel farm, generating plant, or critical communication complex, every effort should be made to establish the 300-foot minimum distance vehicle clearance.

Normally, vehicles will have parking access relatively close to the building installations. If these parking spaces cannot be relocated away from the physical plant, a permit parking procedure will enable some control over the vehicles that do come within close proximity.

In line with control, placing the visitor parking area remote from the building premises will enhance isolation of the threat. It probably will not enhance visitor good will, which may be important if the visitors are customers or potential ones, but this is something that has to be weighed against the increase in security that this type of procedure provides.

If it is possible to park relatively close to a building, the threat of a mobile bomb can be effectively minimized by, again, good lighting and frequent security guard patrols. A bomber is not liable to park a mobile bomb where there is a glaring light or where there is a visible security guard present.

Exterior Building Features

Bushes growing against a building exterior, window wells, structural corners providing concealment, and basement entrances accessible from street level are all favorite places for planting a bomb. The blasts at the Des Moines police department and the Federal Building in Minneapolis are cases in point. Where for esthetics, cost, or ease of access it is not desirable to eliminate such features, it would be advisable to have them inspected frequently as part of the night security patrol.

Interior Areas

A building layout should be structured to maximize the natural physical protection, provided those resources which are critical to operational continuity represent a high value or constitute sensitive energy sources themselves. A computer operation, for

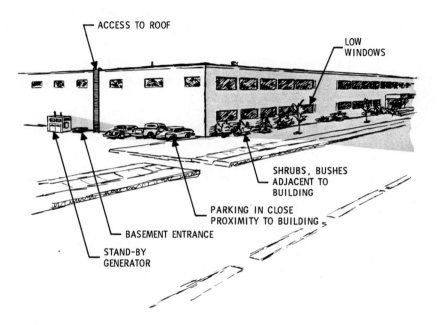

VULNERABLE AREAS

Figure 26

instance, can represent both a high investment and an extremely important element in company functions. It should be located, then, so that it is difficult to get to and/or can be economically guarded.

In multilevel buildings it is preferable to locate critical, costly resources in the top floors. This simplifies the job and the cost of protecting these facility complexes. If a costly, critical installation has been established on a ground or midlevel floor, deterrent controls should be established over adjacent areas as necessary to provide adequate protection.

The extent to which the public has access to the interior of a building is significant in defining a deterrent capability. If complete public access is a necessary condition to the company's business, then it is not so much layout but watchful vigilance that is the most effective deterrent measure. Even here, however, knowledgeable layout or layout modification can enhance the deterrent capability.

The public lavatory is, as noted previously, a favorite place to plant a bomb. There are quite a few business establishments that have closed down their public lavatories, but in many cases this may not be desirable or even possible. If lavatory facilities are regarded as a necessary service for public convenience, consideration should be given to layout modifications should rest rooms be located adjacent to critical, expensive resources. If a public lavatory is next to a computer operation, for instance, one of them should be relocated.

The public sector of an installation should be consolidated insofar as possible. If offices serving the public are scattered throughout a building, it is extremely difficult to develop a protective barrier scheme effective against the bomb threat in the nonpublic areas. Ideally, the public sector is confined to the ground floor and adjacent stories as necessary to provide the required space. Access from the public to the nonpublic areas is, of course, through controlled passage points.

PERSONNEL CONTROL

The use of identification badges for employees as a means of personnel access control within a building is rapidly increasing in popularity. It is, in view of the additional protection provided, a very inexpensive control measure. With the badge system, every employee assumes a security function because every employee will regard with suspicion any person not properly badged. The total effect then is a significant expansion of security consciousness and surveillance at a minimum cost.

This assumes that the person contemplating or attempting explosive violence will be an outsider, an assumption that is valid on the basis of historical evidence. Whether the motive be political or criminal, the mover of the violence has almost invariably been a stranger to the institutional community violated. This excludes the university environment where violence often originates in the student body, and it also excludes corporation violence as a consequence of strike activities.

There is some reluctance on the part of many companies to institute badging because it is viewed as institutional regimentation and/or invasion of personal freedom. I concur with these sentiments and wish devoutly that we did live in a world where every man himself observed those restraints in his actions necessary to the common good.

We do not live in so trusting and comfortable a union, and it therefore really becomes a question not of whether by badging you are abridging the freedom of employees, but whether you are increasing the risk to them by a failure to badge. Badging can deter a bomber, or it can force him to plant on the outside the bomb he would like to place on the inside. This is a consideration that should have significant influence in the decision to institute badging.

While badges may be adopted as a necessary evil, it is not necessary that they be designed without esthetic virture. In the past, industry (and government, too) generally has apparently coalesced around the notion that badges should be drab, colorless, and crowded on the face side, with all the statistical notations that serve to identify a particular individual. In truth, of course, a badge can be attractive and still meet all the requirements of its basic security function.

TRAINING

Training begins not with the security guard or telephone operator but with management at the board and executive officer level. It is necessary that both the makers and implementers of policy at the very top echelons be generally familiar with the institutional and personnel threat of bombs and incendiaries. This information enables them to make knowledgeable budget allowances for security and to express a management awareness and concern that can be effective in increasing the security consciousness of personnel throughout the organization.

The most effective technique for reaching top management is the executive briefing. To be totally productive, however, the briefing should also, after modifications as appropriate, be presented to all levels of middle management. It is here that security policy directives and instructions most frequently break down. The middle manager whose effectiveness is most directly adjudged by a profit curve is not going to consider security matters with the same degree of concern that he brings to a problem of escalating labor cost unless he is made aware of the potential urgency of the situation.

All security personnel should be trained in bomb threat procedures. The objective of this training is to enable them to protect themselves, their fellow employees, and institutional property in the event of a bomb incident. The subjects with which security personnel should be familiar are basically those covered in this book with particular emphasis on identification, evacuation, search, and the action to be taken upon discovery of a bomb or a suspected device.

All other company personnel who are assigned specific functions in the bomb threat situation should be trained in the particular procedure they will employ. Telephone operators, floor wardens having evacuation assignments, and search personnel should be instructed as to their exact duties and how they should be carried out.

Rehearsals

Rehearsal exercises should be arranged periodically to assure a

RECOMMENDED TRAINING

Executive/management	1 hr	Intelligence briefing
Security directors and managers	3 hrs	Threat background Vulnerabilities Deterrence measures Protective measures Legal aspects
Security guards** (Search and evacuation Personnel, fire wardens)	2 hrs	Bomb-incendiary recognition and hazards Evacuation procedures Search procedures
Janitors, maintenance* personnel	1 hr	Bomb-incendiary recognition and hazards
Telephone operators*	1/2 hr	Handling threat calls

*Quarterly
**In addition, should have one practical problem per quarter.

high state of readiness for evacuation and search operations. In evacuation, it is not necessary that all personnel participate in every exercise, but certainly all those assigned evacuation responsibilities should participate.

In evacuation and search practice sessions, it is important to consider the nighttime situation. Too often the evacuation and search problem is considered to be something that can only occur during business hours, even though the evidence clearly reveals that bombings at night are more common. As a consequence, the night shifts are frequently overlooked in evacuation planning, and search teams are not exercised during the hours of darkness. In both planning and rehearsals, the objective should be, of course, to develop a 24-hour a day awareness and readiness.

PROTECTIVE EQUIPMENT

A number of entrepeneurs are offering a variety of devices and equipment for bomb protection to business and industry. The items available include bomb baskets and bomb blankets, electronic stethoscopes, fluoroscopes, armored clothing, and so on. Most of this equipment is effective to a degree when employed by personnel skilled in bomb hazards and hazard control techniques. The key here is *skilled personnel,* and the only ones adequately qualified in this area are law enforcement or military bomb disposal technicians. Lacking such personnel, the equipment generally is not only ineffective but potentially dangerous. The availability of the equipment implies to an unskilled person that he has a capability in dealing with a bomb when in fact he can only obtain such a capability through extensive training and long experience.

There are potential perils even in protective equipment that seems easy to use and effective in performance. One bomb blanket, for instance, is widely advertised as an economical answer to most homemade bombs. Advertising asserts that the blanket can be used by anyone to cover up an explosive device, and that it will reduce up to 90% of the fragmentation. While it is, in fact, capable of containing blast and fragmentation to some extent, its use entails increased human exposure. The possible protection it can provide to property involves an additional risk to human life. This is hardly a justifiable trade-off in most cases.

There are, however, times when such a risk is warranted. If a bomb is located next to an iron lung installation in a hospital, additional human exposure is justified in protecting the life-critical function. Additional risk is also acceptable where a bomb is located next to an energy source, such as a large propance tank, which, as a result of bomb detonation, might considerably amplify the destructive effects and increase the peril to life. However, where the property involved represents money value only, it is hardly worth a human life to try to protect it.

Before investing in any detection or protection equipment, the following questions should be answered:

What specific advantage is provided?

Does use of the equipment entail an additional hazard of some kind? (And if yes, can the additional hazard really be justified on the basis of the specific advantage?)

Do we have personnel technically qualified to use or operate the equipment?

Coping with these questions in detail will provide the type of information needed to determine whether the equipment is useful, usable, or just plain dangerous.

PERSONAL PROTECTION

When an individual person becomes a target, usually his car is booby-trapped or he is attacked in his home. The best protection against a car bomb is to keep the vehicle under 24-hour surveillance, but this is not economically feasible in most cases. An effective alternate is to install a tamper warning device, the kind (sold to deter car thieves) that gives off an audible alarm when a vehicle is disturbed. A simpler approach is to affix small squares of scotch tape at the bottoms of the car doors and at the edge of the hood (at some unobtrusive point). Any entry into the car through these access openings will result in tape disruption, a certain indication to the owner that his car has been tampered with.

None of these measures (except 24-hour surveillance) are absolute safeguards. There are ways to booby-trap a car without disturbing it or even touching it. Most bombers, however, will try to seek access through the hood or a door, and these measures are effective against that type of approach.

Where the target is attacked in his home, most generally a bomb (explosive or incendiary) will be thrown through a window or planted next to the house. The best protection here is, as in the case of premises adjacent to business and industrial buildings, high luminosity exterior lighting.

Occasionally, an explosive device will be sent through the mail to the target. The best protection against this type of attack is to refuse any packages unless the sender is known and it can be verified that he did, in fact, send it.

IV

HAZARD COUNTERMEASURES

PLANNING AND PREPARATION

COUNTERMEASURES are those emergency procedures or provisions that are instituted to protect lives and property in a bomb incident or threat situation. The effectiveness of countermeasures will depend substantially on the completeness and the adequacy of advance planning and preparation. In setting up plans to cope with the bomb emergency, consideration should be given to

1. processing bomb threat communications,
2. evacuation,
3. search.

Prior to initiating countermeasures planning, local law enforcement authorities should be contacted to determine the type and extent of assistance they will be able to provide under various bomb threat conditions. It is probably erroneous to presume that the police will search building premises any time a threat call is received. They usually will, certainly, if it can be accomplished without detriment to their other obligations. When a community is besieged by a wave of bombs and/or bomb threats, all available police resources will normally be too fully occupied with emergency situations to be able to conduct routine searches.

The police will, however, respond immediately any time a bomb or suspected bomb is located. Handling the bomb incident is a recognized responsibility of law enforcement, and most large city departments have a bomb squad capable of taking care of such incidents. While smaller departments may not have bomb disposal personnel, they know where such personnel can be located.

BOMB THREAT COMMUNICATIONS

The telephone is the normal channel for communicating bomb

threats, both actual and hoax. The incidence of hoax calls reaches epidemic proportions when a community or region is undergoing a wave of bombings. There are no complete figures on the ratio of hoax to actual, but what data are available suggest that 100 to 1 is not unrealistic. Obviously, then, a business enterprise should not plan to invoke full emergency measures, including evacuation, every time a bomb threat is received. Obviously, too, no threat should be ignored. If it is authentic, if there actually is a bomb planted, it is quite possible that lives can be saved by appropriate emergency action. Every threat call should therefore be evaluated to determine its credibility as a prerequisite to the decision as to what emergency procedures are appropriate, if any.

The acquisition of as much information about the call as possible is a necessary prerequisite to evaluation. Many companies now provide switchboard personnel with checklists for operators to use in the event of any incoming threat calls. The operator completes, or tries to complete, each item on the list by skillful interrogation of the caller. In addition, operators at most major corporations have been schooled in procedures for notifying the telephone company and instituting a search while the caller is still on the line.

Do not, however, place great reliance on the ability of the phone company to trace calls. It is technologically possible, but practical difficulties make success highly improbable. Even were phone companies able to quickly trace and locate a caller, it would not help in the immediate situation. The majority of threat calls are timed to give a warning of less than an hour before a bomb is supposed to go off. So if a caller is located and apprehended, there will not be time in most cases to interrogate him as to the veracity of the call.

The decision as to emergency action will have to be made on the basis of the telephone evidence. It will help if the call is recorded, and equipment to do this is readily available. The transcription can then be replayed for clues that may help establish or demolish the credibility of the call. Before a final decision is reached, local law enforcement should be consulted. They may well have data on the pattern of telephone threats in the community that may be of assistance in arriving at a decision.

Recommended
Bomb Threat Call
Check List

Date
Time
Transmitted
To

Operator

A. Message

Use exact words as nearly as possible:

B. ID Characteristics

1. Sex M   F   2. Age Group   Under 20   20 to 35   35 to 50   Over 50

3. Mood; Angry   Impatient   Subdued   Determined   Scared

4. Speech Characteristics: note any characteristics including accent which may help to classify the voice by regional or cultural background or by ethnic group

5. Individual Characteristics: indicate any characteristics such as stuttering, slurring, lisping which may be helpful in classifying speech on individual basis

C. Background Noises

No distinguishable background   Music (note type)

Machinery   Traffic   Other (describe)

The decision can range from no action (call adjudged on obvious hoax) to full emergency measures with complete evacuation. The options within these extremes consist of

1. limited search only (check of such popular bomb plant areas as lavatories, stairwells),
2. complete search,
3. limited evacuation and limited or complete search,
4. complete evacuation and complete search.

Whatever decision is reached, the police and the fire department should be notified immediately of the intended action.

EVACUATION

The procedures and control techniques established for the evacaution of a premise in a fire are generally applicable to evacuation in a bomb threat circumstance. The bomb situation, however, does invoke some unique factors, and these should be appropriately considered in adapting a fire evacuation plan to meet the requirements of evacuation in response to a bomb threat.

Notification to Evacuate

Notification procedures should be established and promulgated to all persons involved in the notification chain. Since most procedures will be equipment dependent, alternate techniques for implementation in the event of equipment failure are recommended.

The telephone pyramid is the most direct and controllable method of notification. It also permits the transmission of cautionary or situational information affecting the evacuation, i.e. elevators not operating; use alternate routes. Alarm gongs, bells, or horns should be used with discretion, particularly in multilevel structures, since they generally encourage mass and uncontrolled exodus under circumstances that could result in panic.

Evacuation Routes

Plan to utilize all avenues and means of egress — elevators, escalators, fire escapes, stairwells — in evacuating a building. Some people argue against the use of elevators, noting that a jammed elevator is an ideal situation for panic should a power failure occur (which could be the consequence of a bomb blast), and also that an elevator is itself particularly vulnerable to a bomb plant. Neither of these eventualities has as yet occurred in America, and elevators have been used extensively in evacuation. There have been several instances where a group of police officers in an elevator were subjected to small firebombs dropped on to the cab roof, but harassment seems to have been the intent, and the officers were never actually in any real danger.

It does make sense to use elevators. In some buildings, there are no other means of egress available.

Egress Route Presearch

It also makes sense to verify by presearch that means and avenues of egress (elevators, stairs, hallways) are clear of hazard prior to initiating the movement of personnel. As discussed previously, bombs are frequently planted in those areas (entrance foyers, stairwells, hallways) used for ingress and egress. The presearch of these traffic avenues then becomes an important element in limiting the risk to human life. The plan should provide for alternate routes should a bomb or suspected device be found in one of the designated evacuation avenues.

Search Approaches

ELEVATORS. If manned, conduct search of top of elevator and check shaft for smoke. If unmanned, check interior of elevator, top, and shaft. Assign one person to operate elevator until evacuation is complete.

STAIRWELLS, HALLWAYS. Designate fire wardens or deputies on each floor to search stairwell down to floor below. Floor wardens will then return and initiate evacuation. Hallways to be used for evacuation should be searched concurrently.

Evacuation Control

Floor wardens (with the assistance of department heads and/or supervisors) should undertake full responsibility for orderly, effective evacuation of the people in their areas or organization structures. A check-off procedure should be utilized as a control measure to ensure that all personnel have vacated the premises.

It is advisable to have a responsible person accompany each evacuation group. This ensures continuing control and provides an agent network which can be used to expedite the return movement when the emergency is over.

Security personnel should be posted at critical locations to expedite personnel movement during the evacuation.

Evacuation Perimeter

Merely relocating people from the inside to the outside of a building doesn't necessarily isolate them from potential bomb hazards. In some cases, they may have been removed from a place of relative safety to a location of high peril. There are exterior dangers to be considered as was well illustrated by the New York bomb factory and the Cambridge County Courthouse explosions. In both cases, the detonations resulted in a violent Niagara of masonry and structural debris erupting into the adjacent street. To protect people from this type of hazard, it is necessary to evacuate them far enough from the threatened building to place them outside the perimeter of external hazard.

In downtown sections, law enforcement personnel will institute the necessary controls in outside areas to ensure adequate clearance margins. Where the plant or building and the adjacent premises are company property, institutional security must necessarily undertake the responsibility for moving people far enough from the threatened building to put them beyond the range of the external hazard. The evacuation distance most commonly accepted as adequate is 300 feet. Moving all personnel at least 300 feet from the building will position them outside the hazard zone for most bomb situations.

Recall

When it has been ascertained that a bomb threat no longer exists, economic considerations dictate that personnel should be returned to their operations as quickly as possible. In the isolated plant or building situation, or where the locations to which people have been evacuated are under company control, communicating the recall order is a relatively straightforward task.

In a downtown environment, however, communicating and coordinating a recall can be extremely difficult. The most effective communications approach is to equip floor wardens and/or supervisors-managers with portable radios or paging devices. Word can then be relayed immediately upon the termination of the emergency condition. The least effective communication technique is to require that personnel in charge of evacuation groups call in to a central switchboard periodically. Experience shows that during and following bomb incidents, telephone channels to the outside world are so impossibly jammed that even high priority emergency traffic cannot get through.

SEARCH

The objective of the search is to determine whether an explosive or incendiary device has been planted on the premises and, if so, to isolate it until it can be neutralized by qualified personnel. The preplanning steps consist of identifying search team members, assigning areas or zones of responsibility to teams, and training team personnel to ensure their operational effectiveness. In assigning search responsibilities, a sequence of priorities should be followed.

Search Priorities

Search priorities should be defined as part of the search plan on the basis of the order of preference in places for hiding a bomb. Public access areas should receive immediate attention, and then the effort should be directed to institutionally private sectors. If the institution owns or controls the adjacent outside areas, an exterior search should be made in parallel with the interior effort.

In setting up priorities, it is wise to consider resources that are unique to the corporation as previously discussed. The critical function, the installation-facility of substantial value, the potentially destructive energy sources all demand priority attention. The necessity of extensive or detailed search in these areas is diminished, of course, in direct relation to the effectiveness of routine protective measures.

Formation and Deployment

Search teams should be structured and deployed to limit the possible hazard to the personnel involved as much as possible. This means, first of all, minimum-sized search teams. It is a gross stupidity to send a six or eight man search group into a room to look for a bomb since this maximizes the number of people exposed to potential hazards. Should a bomb detonate during a search, there is probable justification if one or even possibly two search personnel are exposed to the effects. But never more, never six or eight.

One-man teams (a contradiction in terms but appropriately descriptive) are ideal, although circumstances usually dictate two — a person familiar with the area and another, normally a security guard, able to recognize an explosive device and schooled in protective measures. Where two are used, they should between themselves maintain a maximum separation by searching in different parts of the assigned room or area. This increases the probability that only one person will be exposed to hazardous effects if a device should explode.

The principle of maximum separation extends also to deployment of teams. Search teams should be assigned areas in a location sequence ensuring that there is maximum clearance between the various groups. Where multilevel buildings are involved, floors should be searched simultaneously.

TWO MAN SEARCH PATTERNS

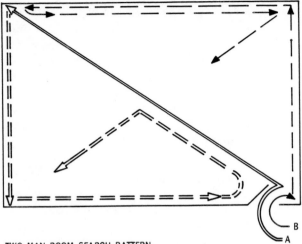

TWO-MAN ROOM SEARCH PATTERN

"A" GOES DIRECTLY TO FAR CORNER AND STARTS SEARCHING
AROUND ROOM WHILE "B" STARTS AT CORNER NEXT TO DOOR. WHEN
AREAS NEXT TO WALLS HAVE BEEN SEARCHED, "A" MOVES TO CENTER
OF ROOM AND SEARCHES OUTWARD, "B" MOVES TO CORNER AND
SEARCHES TOWARD CENTER. THIS APPROACH KEEPS SEARCH
PERSONNEL SEPARATED AS FAR AS POSSIBLE.

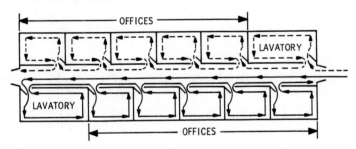

FLOOR SEARCH

SEARCH PERSONNEL FOLLOW A PATTERN WHICH IS CONSISTENT WITH
MAXIMUM SEPARATION AT ALL TIMES.

Figure 27

Communications

There must be some reliable form of communication between the control center and the search parties, particularly where the building or premises to be searched are large or structurally complex. Ready communications enables not only continuing coordination of the search effort but rapid notification to the control center if a device is discovered.

Radio is the most convenient form of communication in the search situation. However, some sources caution against the use of radios in a bomb search, pointing out that the RF energy associated with radio transmissions can activate an electric blasting cap, which may be used in a bomb explosive train. This is true, but the circumstances under which inadvertent initiation can occur are unique and not likely to be duplicated in a bomb incident. For a potential danger to exist, the blasting cap leads would have to be configured into an antenna and have to be properly oriented to intercept the transmission, and this would not be typical of normal bomb construction.

The average portable radio operating on the citizen's band (26.96 to 27.23MHz) and at a power of 5 watts represents very little hazard in this regard. The Institute of Makers of Explosives Safety Pamphlet No. 20 indicates that such a radio can be operated as close as 5 feet to an electric cap without any danger of inadvertent initiation; of course, that danger would only exist if the cap lead wires were formed into an effective and properly oriented antenna.

Radios with the proper power and transmission frequency characteristics are, then, safe and should be used. As a prudent safeguard, however, it is probably wise that search personnel employ these radios in hallways only and not carry them into rooms to be investigated. With this precaution, the possibility that a bomb could be inadvertently triggered by radio transmissions is essentially zero.

Bomb Identification

The searchers should, obviously, know what they are searching for. Personnel assigned to search responsibilities should therefore be given advance training in bomb recognition. The devices illustrated in this book are typical of devices that have been used, and searchers should be familiar with these configurations. However, it it important to understand that typical, in this regard, should not be considered as restricting. Explosive devices have, in fact, been assembled in almost every conceivable physical shape and appearance. Bombs have been packaged in paper sacks, books, laundry bags, tin cans, bottles, light bulbs, and so on.

Searchers should be instructed that they are looking for anything that is alien to its immediate environment. This includes the typical devices previously discussed and anything else that is recognized, by instinct or intuition, as something that does not belong in the circumstances in which it is located.

Action When Device Is Located

In 1917, a suspected package was removed from a Milwaukee post office and taken to the nearest police precinct station. There while it was being examined, it exploded and killed nine officers and two civilians. Retrospect confers on us a wondrous wisdom, and in this advantage of hindsight we might look back and remark how stupid it was for eleven people to congregate in close proximity to a package already determined to be suspicious. But without an awareness of the potential hazards of such a package, any one of us might have been caught in those particular circumstances. However, now we know the hazards of bomb devices, and we appreciate, therefore, the necessity of prudent action in a bomb incident.

When something is located that is identified as a bomb or suspected bomb, search personnel should immediately evacuate the area and set up a perimeter of control around the device. The police authorities should be notified, and no one should be permitted in the vicinity until the police have investigated and taken appropriate action.

It is important to emphasize that search personnel should not linger in the vicinity nor attempt any disarm procedures, regardless of the appearance of the bomb or suspected bomb. To do otherwise invites disaster. As evident in the discussion on bomb technology, target-activated type instruments can be initiated by the slightest jar or movement, or even, with some fuzing techniques, if they are approached. Time delay mechanisms could time out and fire at any moment.

Some bombs may have exterior characteristics which can create the impression that the device could be safed by some simple, direct action. Electrical wiring could be exposed, for instance, and it might be concluded that cutting a wire would break the circuit and make it impossible to function. Or a piece of time fuse extending to the exterior of the device could tempt direct action, i.e. removal of the fuse, as a means of rendering the device safe. But the exposed wire or external fuse could be a ruse, a decoy designed specifically to elicit the type of action which then triggers the real fuzing mechanism. This is a bombing technique that has been used in the past and can be expected in the future.

It is important, then, that search personnel be specifically instructed that under no circumstances do they ever touch, move, or tamper with a suspected device, regardless of the circumstances.

V

EDUCATIONAL INSTITUTIONS

IN the context of the bomb and incendiary threat, the educational community occupies a unique position. Next to police departments and federal buildings, schools and universities are the most popular of targets, yet they are generally not compatible either physically or operationally with the type of safeguards necessary to effectively deter the threat or protect against it. And quite commonly, at least at the university level, the enemy lives inside the house. It is very difficult to protect against a bomber who has a privileged sanctuary within the institution itself.

The scope of the attack on schools across the nation generally has not been appreciated. There were over 150 bombing incidents involving schools in the first 9 months of 1970 alone. Nor were these bombings confined to institutions of higher learning. Many of the targets were at the junior and senior high school levels, and some were even elementary schools, such as Lorton Elementary in Lorton, Virginia, which sustained damage estimated at two hundred thousand dollars in a firebombing attack. It is not any one level of school, then, that is susceptible to explosive and incendiary violence, but the entire educational community.

In establishing a protective capability against bombs and incendiaries, school officials should consider the deterrence and protective procedures discussed elsewhere in this book and also the distinctive nature of their own institutions. Schools differ widely in their operational styles and environmental circumstances, but generally, at least insofar as bomb protection is concerned, there are two basic situations: that found in academic institutions up through high schools and that characteristic of universities and colleges.

ELEMENTARY AND HIGH SCHOOLS

Because these schools normally do not have organic police or security personnel, principals and system superintendents must depend on local law enforcement organizations for protection against the bomb threat. The police are able and willing to provide assistance in drafting procedures for handling warning telephone calls, evacuation, and search. They will also, in most cases, conduct search operations themselves. To capitalize fully on this police aid, it is important that law enforcement officials be contacted early in the planning stages and that clear agreement be reached on the extent of their participation in a bomb emergency.

Telephone Calls

The procedure for handling threat telephone calls discussed elsewhere in this book can be adapted (with modifications as may be recommended by local police) directly for school use. Schools, however, generally do not as a prerequisite to further action go through the process of analyzing calls for credibility. The decision in most cases is automatic: complete evacuation and full search whenever a call is received. The reason is quite simple. Should children be injured as a consequence of a failure to evacuate following a warning, it would be pretty difficult to explain to the community at large generally and to the parents involved particularly why evacuation was not ordered.

Yet school authorities know that most warning calls are hoaxes perpetrated by students who want to avoid some school activity or who simply enjoy the furore and excitement an emergency evacuation engenders. It has been found that these hoax calls can be sharply reduced if the school establishes a policy of equal make-up (on an off day preferably) for any time lost because of a false bomb report. When such a policy is widely publicized, students quickly lose interest in this type of diversion.

Evacuation

The fire evacuation procedure is appropriate for use in bomb threat situations provided two important modifications are made. The procedure should be revised first to provide for a careful presearch of all egress routes before evacuation movement is initiated and second to ensure that the holding area to which students move is far enough from buildings so that there is no danger from flying debris.

Search

Schools should have a search capability to the extent required to determine whether egress routes are clear before an evacuation is initiated. This can be done by assigning a few faculty and/or maintenance personnel to this activity as part of the evacuation plan. However, setting up formal, well trained and equipped search teams is neither necessary nor desirable except in cases where the police cannot undertake search responsibility. In all other instances, school planning should focus on assisting rather than duplicating the police effort. Assistance can be provided by designating staff personnel as guides to the police where necessary.

Standing Security

The objective of standing security is to minimize opportunities for planting a bomb or incendiary device on school premises and to increase the probability that if a device is planted, it will be readily located. This objective can best be achieved by limiting access to all parts of school buildings to personnel who have a need for access based on legitimate job functions. The effectiveness of standing security can be significantly enhanced if all faculty, administrative, and maintenance personnel exercise continuing surveillance as part of their normal duties and promptly report any occurrence which reflects a deviation from normal circumstances and/or customary practices.

All boiler rooms, cleaning and maintenance spaces, and other such areas that are used for storage or school building support should be kept locked at all times except when authorized personnel are in these areas. A procedure to limit the availability of keys to such rooms should be established.

A complete inspection of buildings and premises should be made each school day before classes convene in the morning and after classes are completed in the afternoon. In addition, additional inspections can best be made by designated representatives of the maintenance staff.

COLLEGES AND UNIVERSITIES

Colleges and universities have institutional characteristics that differ sharply from those of the lower level schools. Universities have organic police forces, students in residence, and usually large campuses with many buildings. The student body is, also, a much more volatile population than that of grammar or high schools.

Some of the procedures described for elementary and high schools are appropriate for the university and should be adopted. However, the university police and the maintenance staff offer personnel resources that can be tapped to increase the protective capability.

University Police

Whether the university police should have a bomb squad depends on local conditions. If the university is large, is frequently disrupted by violence, and is not so situated that it can be readily served by an existing city or armed services bomb disposal unit, then a university squad is highly recommended. Without one, the campus is virtually defenseless against a very real threat to life and property.

Establishing a bomb disposal capability is not easy. It takes money (a fluoroscopic inspection device alone costs about $5,000), and there are very few places where the requisite training is offered. To assign bomb disposal responsibilities to someone without providing adequate training (it takes at least 3 weeks in a full-time course) is to create an extremely dangerous situation.

The training can be bypassed by hiring already qualified personnel — retired or ex-servicemen who are graduates of the Explosive Ordnance Disposal School at Indianhead, Maryland. These people are fully competent to disarm and dispose of any explosive or incendiary device.

Whether or not a bomb squad is organized on the campus, it is important that all campus police be trained in bomb reconnaissance, which covers device recognition, hazards, and hazard control procedures. Not only is such training necessary to enable the police to protect students and faculty, it is essential to their own protection. The campus police, their headquarters, their cars, and even their homes, are frequently targets for explosive and incendiary violence.

Maintenance Personnel

Probably no single group of individuals knows the physical idiosyncrasies of the campus quite so intimately as the maintenance personnel. They are also the ones who are best able to ensure that standing security provisions are enforced, that limited access is maintained over machinery spaces and storage rooms, and that periodic inspections are conducted in classrooms, halls, stairways, and lavatories. To enable them to effectively function in this way, maintenance personnel should be trained in bomb and incendiary recognition and hazards.

It is also advisable that volunteer maintenance personnel be trained in search procedures. They can augment the police to reduce the time required to complete a search or to conduct a search themselves if available police resources are committed to other emergency missions.

VI

THE HOSPITAL, A SPECIAL CASE

MOST hospital managers and administrators are acutely concerned today about the bomb threat as related to their institutions. The cause of their apprehension springs out of the unique and formidable problems peculiar to the hospital situation in the context of a bomb threat. It is not possible to completely evacuate most hospital complexes. Some patients cannot be moved because of their physical condition, some because they are life-sustained by fixed and immovable equipment. Further, closing an emergency operating room, as would be necessary in a complete evacuation, could spell death for a gravely injured patient who was even then on his way to surgery.

In terms of vulnerability, then, the hospital is the most sensitive of targets. There is just no way it can completely protect its patients and ensure the continuity of its life-critical functions.

However, a hospital is not a valid revolutionary target. Mad though they be, revolutionaries are not about to stigmatize their cause by planting a bomb in a hospital. If they are not dissuaded by their own humane instincts, they are deterred by the revolutionary material they so avidly read. Both Che and Mao, at least by implication, place hospitals outside the realm of legitimate targets.

There is, then, no threat from the revolutionary, but there is from the consequences of his influence. The revolutionary has popularized the bomb and the incendiary as effective weapons, and psychotics and criminals have been impressed. Today the apolitical psychotic, the twisted mind seeking revenge for some real or imagined grievance, is much more liable to use this type of device than he was in the past. Criminals, also, are turning increasingly to bombs and incendiaries in robbery, in intimidation, and in blackmail. A hospital is a possible target for attack from these two sources: an ex-patient, for instance, who is psycho-

83

pathically siezed and with the notion that hospital surgery cost him his potency or the addict who sees in the hospital pharmacy a great reservoir of the drugs he so desperately needs.

The possibility is there. It is not so prevalent as most administrators fear, but it is there. And with reasonable prudence and planning, it can be minimized. The steps necessary for effective protection are neither expensive nor complex. They integrate rather nicely with normal security precautions.

The measures for protection and deterrence discussed elsewhere in this book can be applied with appropriate modifications to the hospital situation. The modifications should be coupled with compensatory protective safeguards. In areas where patients can't be evacuated, for example, the search must be immediate and thorough, and there must be some type of shielding (like the Davis Bomb Blanket) available. In other words, if the patient can't be moved, a more comprehensive effort must be made to discover any threat against him, and there should be some way to protect him from any threat discovered.

Energy resources, such as oxygen tanks, should be kept in locked storerooms. When a tank is in use on the floor, it should be so located that a nurse or orderly will have general surveillance over it.

Limited access should be provided for all critical functions and areas. This includes ORs, postop setups, lung, heart, and kidney machine installations, power generating and transmission complexes, and, of course, pharmaceutical storage facilities.

With these measures, you will have attained an effective level of protection for your patients and staff. The revolutionary is not liable to make a hospital his target, and the historical experience supports this conclusion. The psychotic and the criminal might very well, but even this threat, taken in statistical perspective, is minor. An accidental oxygen tank explosion is probably a much more likely contingency than a bomb in surgery. So, though the hospital is the most vulnerable of targets, it is the least susceptible.

INDEX

A

Accidents, explosive, 9
Amatol, 20
Ammonium nitrate, 8, 9, 53
Amonal, 20
Anti-disturbance switch, 37

B

Badges, personnel, 60, 61
Bean bomb, 32, 34
Black Panthers, 5
Black powder, 16, 24
Blast bomb, 42
Blaster's Handbook, 8
Blasting accessories, 20
Blasting caps, 20-23, 26, 27
Bomb
   action when located, 76-77
   blast, 42
   car 12
   construction, 14-47
   destructive capability, 48-49
   employment, 48-52
   fuzing, 28-39
   identification, 75-76
   main charges, 41-42
   man-carried, 48
   mobile, 52-56
Bomb blankets, 64, 84
Bomb fuzing
   remote controlled, 41
   target activated, 28-34
   time delay, 34-39
   types, 28
Bomb squad
   availability, 66
   establishment of, 81
   Montreal incident, 52-53
Bombings

Bank of America, 12
Cambridge County Court House, 71
Chase Manhattan Bank, 12
Compton, California, 14
Dayton's, Minnesota, 50
Des Moines Chamber of Commerce, 50
Des Moines Police Department, 58
Dow Chemical, 12
General Electric, 12
General Motors, 52
Haymarket Square, 12
IBM, 12
Kent, Ohio, 12
Lorton, Virginia, 78
Los Angeles Times Building, 52
Madison, Wisconsin, 48
Milwaukee Police Department, 76
Minneapolis Federal Building, 58
Montreal Canada, 52
New York, 12, 46, 71
   school, 78
Sears Roebuck, 12
University of Wisconsin, 9, 53
U. S. Capitol, 12
Booby traps, 37, 42, 65
Building
   damage vulnerability, 49
   protection, 55-60
   vulnerable features, 58

C

Car bombs, 12, 37, 39
Clockwork bombs, 30-32
Clothspin bombs, 34
Communications, search situation, 75
Comp. B, 20
C-3, C-4, 19
Countermeasures, protective
   evacuation, 69-72
   options, 69

planning and preparation, 66
search, 72-74
Cuba, 7, 9

D

Damage capabilities, bomb, 48-49
Detonating cord, 24-25
Dynamite, 17, 52, 53

E

Electric blasting caps, 21, 75
Elementary schools, 78-81
Evacuation
control, 71
decision, 76, 69, 79
notification, 69
perimeter, 71
pre-search, 70
recall, 72
routes, 69, 70
schools, 79
Explosives
amatol, 20
ammonium nitrate, 8, 9, 53
amonal, 20
black powder, 16, 24
Comp. B, 20
C-3, C-4, 19
dynamite, 17, 52, 53
Explosive D, 17
high, 17-20
lead azide, 17
low, 15-17
Nitramon, 18
nitroglycerine, 17, 19
PETN, 20
plastic, 19
RDX, 19
smokeless powder, 8, 16
tetryl, 20
Explosives, availability of, 8-9
Explosive reactions, 15-16

F

Fencing protection, 55-56
Firing trains, 25-28

Fragmentation bombs, 42
Fuse, 24-26, 28, 30

H

High explosives, 17-20
High schools, 79-81
Hoax telephone calls, 67
Hoover, J. Edgar, 5
Hospitals, 83-85

I

Ice cube bombs, 32
Incendiaries, Molotov cocktail, 42-48
Information, bomb construction, 7

L

Lead azide, 17
Lighting, protective, 55
Low explosives, 15-17

M

Management briefing, 62
Mercury switches, 37
Military explosives, 20
Mobile bombs, 52, 56
Molotov cocktail, 44
Mousetrap bombs, 37

N

New Left Notes, 7
Nitramon, 18
Nitroglycerine, 17, 19
Non-electric blasting cap, 21

P

Personnel
badging, 60-61
protection, 65
training, 62-63
PETN (explosive), 20
Pipe bombs, 15, 42-43
Planning and preparation, 66
Plastic explosives, 19

Police
  assistance, 66
  bomb responsibility, 76
  university, 81
Protection
  buildings, 55-60
  hospitals, 83-84
  personal, 65
  schools, 78-83
Protective equipment, 63-64
  bomb blanket, 64
  fluoroscope, 64, 81
  stethescope, 64

Q

Quicksilver Times, 7

R

Radios
  use of in search, 75
  use of in evacuation recall, 72
Rehearsal exercise, 62-63
Remote controlled bombs, 39-41
Revolutionary,
  rationale 9-11
  resources 6-9
  threats 3-6

S

SDS, 5-7
Search
  communications, 75

elevators, 70
police assistance, 66
priorities, 72
schools, 80
stairs, hallways, 70
team deployment, 73-74
team size 73
Solenoid delay bombs, 34
Susceptibility to violence, 11-13

T

Telephone
  call checklist, 68
  hoax calls, 67
  operator training, 62
  school threats, 79
  use in evacuation, 69
Tetryl, 20
Time delay fuzes, 28-34
TNT, 17, 20
Training, 62-63

V

Violence
  documentation of, 3
  susceptibility to, 11-13
  threat of, 3-11

W

Wall Street bombing, Preface
Washington Daily News, 7

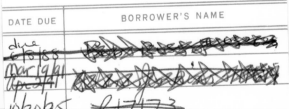